Your Family Voyage

Your Family Voyage

Discover How the Patterns Set by Your Family of Origin Affect Your Life Today

P. Roger Hillerstrom

Fleming H. Revell
A Division of Baker Book House
Grand Rapids, Michigan 49516

Published by Fleming H. Revell,
a division of Baker Book House Company
P.O. Box 6287, Grand Rapids, Michigan 49516-6287

Printed in the United States of America

Library of Congress Cataloging-in-Publication Data

Hillerstrom, Roger.
    Your family voyage : discover how the patterns set by your family of origin affect your life today / Roger Hillerstrom.
        p.   cm.
    Includes bibliographical references.
    ISBN 0-8007-1679-5
    1. Family—Psychological aspects. 2. Family—Religious life. I. Title.
HQ518.H55   1993
306.85—dc20   93-6601

Scripture quotations are from the New American Standard Bible, © the Lockman Foundation 1960, 1962, 1963, 1968, 1971, 1972, 1973, 1975, 1977.

"Family Tradition" by Hank Williams Jr. used by permission of Bocephus Music, Inc. BMI, c/o Dave Burgess Enterprises, P.O. Box 40929, Nashville, TN 37204.

Quotation from the book *Unfinished Business* by Charles Sell, copyright 1989 by Multnomah Press. Published by Multnomah Press, Portland, OR 97266. Used by permission.

Quotation from *Co-Dependency: An Emerging Issue* by various authors, copyright date 1984, reprinted with the permission of the publishers: Health Communications, Inc., Deerfield Beach, Florida.

This book is dedicated to our three delightful children:

Karlyn, our curious and creative firstborn

Lukas, our energetic and insightful secondborn

Rebekah, our adventurous and expressive lastborn

These three precious gems are a constant source
of joy and wonder to their mom and dad.
It is truly a privilege to be a part of their family of origin.

Contents

A Word of Thanks

Completing a book like this is a monumental task, certainly beyond my abilities. God has graciously filled my life with people whose skills, abilities, and generosity have made this work possible. All of them have earned my respect and gratitude.

My wife, Beth. Without her support, encouragement, and sacrifice I could never have gotten beyond a title.

Elaine Colvan, director of the Christian Writer's Network. Her editorial insight has shaped this work from the proposal to the final chapter.

H. Norman Wright, for his insight, experience, and consistent encouragement.

Evelyn Bence, for her editorial insight and experience.

My dear friends Mark and Andrea Robertson, whose own family voyages have added so much to the direction of this work.

My parents, Per and Gully Hillerstrom, and my in-laws, Erwin and Betty Neese, for their prayer support and perpetual applause.

Pat and Marilyn Mitchell, who provided an escape for some very intensive and productive time.

Eldon and Andrew Berg, whose technical knowledge has streamlined this work tremendously.

Keith and Genevive Bell, whose insights have added so much to the work.

Our Tuesday night Bible study group, for their prayers, their encouragement, their friendship, and their sincere interest in a very tedious project.

My colleagues and friends at the Crista Counseling Service, whose spiritual and professional commitment are always an inspiration to me.

My extended family at Northshore Baptist Church, who are a constant source of fellowship, insight, and laughter.

How to Use This Book

I wrote this book for you—an adult who grew up in a family system of any kind: a "traditional" family of father, mother, and siblings; a "broken" home with a stepparent and stepsiblings; a single-parent home; or even an institution or a series of foster homes.

Some of you find little fault with the care you received as a child; others of you can hardly bring yourselves to think of the pain you endured. No matter how you remember those early years, they have influenced who you are today.

As you read this book I trust you will have a new understanding of how your family of origin has made you who you are—for good and for bad. On this journey through the past you'll discover how you can take full advantage of the positive effects of your family history as you work to overcome the negative ones.

At the end of each chapter you'll find questions that will help you discover and sort through your past. To answer these questions and to take notes as you read, I suggest you have a notebook at hand. Consider diagramming your family genogram as outlined in the Appendix. This will help you summarize a great deal of information briefly and concisely. To digest what you read and apply it to your family situation, you might want to read no more than a chapter a day. If you do read the book straight through, go back and read it again, spending considerable time "exploring" each concept. Discuss your findings with a close friend or loved one.

If you approach this family journey with an open mind and a desire to discover, I guarantee that you will grow to become more like the man or woman God designed you to be. You're in for a fascinating treasure hunt—enjoy!

1

You Mean All This Stuff Is Mine?

Unseen factors live in our past.
Some are positive, healthy characteristics
that deserve all the energy we can give
them to help them grow and develop.
Some are stumbling blocks that keep us
from experiencing life at its best.
Often we have no idea they even exist!

My wife and I are in recovery—we are recovering pack-rats. Slowly and painfully, we're learning to discard unnecessary material objects. It hasn't been easy. And as with most recoveries, ours began with a crisis.

Recently, Beth and I discovered carpenter ants in our house. It seemed no big deal: We called several exterminators, got some bids, decided on a professional, and set a date for him to come.

But to prepare for the exterminator, we had to empty our attic. What began as a nuisance ended as a horrendous task. Our plan was to simply carry down our "memorabilia" from the attic and place it in a corner of our family room until the exterminator's job was done. It wasn't quite that easy. As we watched our family room fill to capacity, we were absolutely amazed by the mountains of "stuff" that had been slowly accumulating over our heads month after month. We set pile next to pile until the room was completely filled.

There we were, our family room crammed with who knows what from who knows where since who knows when. We concluded that such family debris must somehow breed and reproduce. Since neither of us recognized some of this stuff, we decided it must have been second- or third-generation junk. So much for our treasured memorabilia.

It was then and there that we made a mutual decision. "We will not live through this twice," we said. At this turning point in our lives we began "the purge."

For days we worked. Our conversations were transformed by our new priorities:

"Get rid of it!"

"I can't believe we still have this!"

"When will we *ever* use this?"

"When in doubt, throw it out!"

Occasionally one of us would say, "Well, let's wait on that. We can always throw that away later." (Complete recovery doesn't happen all at once!)

Our labor produced truckloads of donations for our church garage sale and a remarkably organized and well-managed attic—and a new perspective on accumulating material objects.

Our attic was an excellent example of how we all tend to accumulate "baggage" in life. Although we had always been aware that there was "stuff" up there, we had naïvely minimized its proportions. Since the accumulation had been gradual, we were unaware of its size and significance.

In a very similar way we accumulate emotional baggage. During childhood we pick up assumptions, perceptions, reactions, and habits and carry them with us into adulthood. We may be vaguely aware that these have an effect on us, but we minimize their impact.

As a therapist, I am constantly asked questions by people seeking practical answers:

Why do I procrastinate?
Why am I so critical of myself?
What makes it so difficult for me to express feelings?
Why do I constantly seek the approval of others?
Why is it so hard for me to trust others . . . or myself?
What causes me to feel guilty for no apparent reason?
Why am I so easily manipulated by others?

The answers to questions such as these may lie in your "attic"; in the accumulation of "stuff" that you have carried with you since childhood.

I'd like to invite you to take a journey with me through the pages of this book. Together we will travel into your family's history and explore your emotional "attic"—that room full of "stuff" you didn't even know you had kept. It's an expedition—an exploration, a treasure hunt—that will immeasurably enrich your life.

Is This Trip Necessary?

Some people will ask, "Is a trip like this important?" The answer is a resounding "yes" from thousands who have taken this journey before you. Its value lies in the fact that our actions are often really *reactions* to factors we may not be able to see. We constantly respond to our environment in myriad ways: When something happens around us we adapt, adjust, attack, or escape, depending on the situation. Our reactions are powerfully influenced by perceptions, emotions, and reflexes that may have little or no connection to our current situation. These unseen factors live in our past. Some are positive, healthy characteristics that deserve all the energy we can give to help them grow and develop. Some are stumbling blocks that keep us from experiencing life at its best. These often stifle our relationships, deaden our marriages, and stunt our growth.

Many people say, "I have no reason to explore my past. I was happy as a child and still am. I can understand sorting through the past for someone who was abused, abandoned, or deeply hurt in some way, but not for me. My childhood just doesn't affect me today."

If this is your view, you are in for some pleasant, even exciting surprises. We are all products of our pasts. Both positive and negative experiences have influenced us in hundreds of ways. Exploring your family of origin will not only aid you in resolving problems, but it will also help you to appreciate your strengths and capitalize on them. It will deepen your insights and broaden your understanding. You will make new discoveries, uncover details you've never considered, and encounter visitors you've never seen. Regardless of where you've been or where you're headed, this trip will change you.

Other people admit their past was fraught with difficulties, but they ask, "Shouldn't we just forget them and move on? After all, according to 2 Corinthians 5:17, when we are in Christ, old things have passed away. Since we are new creatures, the past shouldn't affect us any more." My response to this is generally, "Well, it's usually not quite that simple."

Second Corinthians 5:17 is translated this way in the New American Standard Version: "Therefore if any man is in Christ, he is a new creature; the old things passed away; behold, new things have come." In Christ we have the power to overcome the negative past and its resulting undesirable character traits. The cross gives us the potential to replace our old ways with positive, healthy patterns. But nowhere does the Bible teach that this process is automatic. For change to occur, we must commit ourselves to it, make conscious decisions regarding problem areas, and apply biblical principles to deal with them.

Certainly some individuals have overcome struggles with their past easily and instantly, with no conscious effort. I call these miracles, because they go directly against what is normal and predictable in human functioning. Such instantaneous change can be attributed to God's sovereign intervention, not to a human decision to ignore the problem. By definition a miracle is rare, uncontrollable, and unexpected.

In most instances, just letting the "junk" accumulate in the attic isn't an option. The floorboards start to buckle and the mildew starts to smell. We may be able to convince ourselves that the problems are gone, but they continue to haunt us. Remember the apostle Paul's admonition in 1 Corinthians 10:12: "Therefore let him who thinks he stands take heed lest he fall."

Before we move ahead, we need to prepare for our journey. Many of the discoveries we make may surprise and confuse us, so we'll need a general idea of how to proceed. To begin, let's look at the experience of someone who has already taken this voyage.

The Voyage of Bob: A Child at Mid-Life

As his forty-seventh birthday approached, Bob lived a comfortable life. A vice president of a prospering midsized company, he worked with a highly skilled management team and enjoyed the relationships with his co-workers a great deal. His two children were out of college and successful. His wife, Betty, had returned to her nursing career five years earlier and was doing well. Together they earned a more-than-comfortable income. Both Bob and Betty were Christians who took their faith seriously. Active in their church, they surrounded themselves with Christian friends who held similar spiritual values.

In spite of all this, Bob was deeply discontented. He was increasingly cross and negative with Betty, and his co-workers were finding him abrasive and difficult to work with. When he began to contemplate having an affair with his secretary, he "woke up," startled and confused. An extramarital affair was totally against his values as a Christian and had never before crossed his mind. Even more confusing was the fact that he did not find this woman particularly attractive, and her personality generally irritated him—yet he found himself drawn to her in a strange, yet compelling way. This emotional attraction to his secretary finally brought Bob to my office. While in therapy, Bob took a long look at himself and sorted through his emotional development.

Bob was raised in a Christian home where he was loved and cared for. Although his parents never expressed a great deal of emotional warmth, there wasn't much conflict in the home, either. He considered his childhood happy and well adjusted.

As the eldest of three children, Bob was familiar with responsibility long before he reached adulthood. In many ways he took care of his younger sister and brother and was a good role model for them. His sister had a particularly difficult adolescence, struggling with drugs and alcohol, and Bob was very involved in helping her during those years.

The family's expectations for Bob were high, but he met them consistently. In his family he had taken on a "hero" role: He was the successful, responsible, firstborn son.

Betty was still in high school when she married Bob. She had been a friend of Bob's sister, and he related to her in much the same way he related to his younger siblings. Betty admired Bob and enjoyed the attention and nurturance he offered.

As children came and life moved on, Bob did what needed to be done, just as he always had. Professionally, socially, and personally, success naturally seemed to follow him. Lately, however, something seemed to be changing, and it confused him. Logically he should have been more content than ever before. All of his well-laid plans were now in place and life was cruising along as he had always hoped it would, but he still wasn't satisfied.

As Bob explored his family of origin he made some amazing discoveries about himself. He began to recognize an underlying message he had received from his family: His value and acceptance were based on his performance and behavior. As his journey progressed, he eventually recalled several incidents in which he had failed to perform to his usual standards. The family's message of rejection had been subtle but clear. Since he had been the family success, he had consistently received the acceptance and had never had to question or evaluate it.

Bob also discovered that his family had taught him to ignore his emotions and focus on his behavior. Throughout his life, when strong feelings arose he quickly became confused. Having no idea what to do with feelings, he would usually just work harder until they went away.

The most significant discovery for Bob was that he had spent his entire life rescuing and taking care of others. In hundreds of subtle ways he had been taught that his worth came from his ability to help others out of trouble. Now at forty-seven, he had no one to rescue or care for. Though very successful, he had a nagging sense of failure. Bob also began to see that part of his attraction to his secretary was that she had many personal problems and was a very emotionally dependent person.

Bob's voyage through his past led him to take a long, hard look at his concept of God. He found that his experience of God was tightly wrapped up in his experience with his parents. He had projected parental expectations and responses onto God. For example, though Bob intellectually understood God's love and forgiveness, he lived with a deep sense of guilt and disapproval. Even though his lifestyle was consistent with his spiritual values and God had blessed his obedience, his emotional response was always the same. On this journey, Bob discovered that his spiritual activity was motivated by a fear of rejection by God, rather than a response to God's love. He had spent his life running *from* God's wrath rather than *to* God's acceptance and love.

With this new insight, Bob spent hours in study, learning about God's grace and acceptance. Slowly the truth of God's unconditional love began to make sense to him. He learned to separate his parents' imperfection from God's perfection. In discovering God's grace he found a peace and contentment he'd never known.

As a result of his journey, Bob found the freedom to make a number of decisions. Some patterns from the past he decided to set aside and discard; some he decided to keep and develop. Most significantly, he resigned his corporate position and took a lower-paying administrative job at a local children's hospital. This was a career in which his care-taking role could be fully expressed. It was also a position in which Betty, as a nurse, could take an active interest. The prospect of sharing this new part of their lives brought them much closer. Bob felt exhilarated by the thought of the future.

As is typical of people who take this journey, when Bob first began recognizing some of these old patterns, his initial impulse was to focus blame on his parents. As children do, he looked for someone who had failed him or done him wrong in some way. As his exploration progressed, he realized that it wasn't quite that simple. Through his many discoveries, Bob found his parents to be loving, caring individuals, with histories all their own, neither one perfect. He reviewed memories of thoughtful conversations as a teen and meaningful times with each of them— experiences he hadn't thought of for years. Recalling them now as an adult, he saw them with insight he hadn't been capable of as a child. To his amazement, Dad and Mom became much less villainous. He also found that as an adult he was free to change himself in any way he chose.

God's Response to Our Family Histories

Deuteronomy 11:18–21 is a familiar passage that holds a wealth of insight into family life:

> You shall therefore impress these words of mine on your heart and on your soul; and you shall bind them as a sign on your hand, and they shall be as frontals on your forehead. And you shall teach them to your sons, talking of them as you sit in your house and when you walk along the road and when you lie down and when you rise up. And you shall write them on the doorposts of your house and on your gates, so that your days and the days of your sons may be multiplied on the land which the LORD swore to your fathers to give them, as long as the heavens remain above the earth.

In this passage God is saying far more than, "Teach your children my commandments." He says, "Build your family's world around my Word. Allow my commandments to become the environment your children grow up in, and future generations will be blessed." The reason behind the admonition is this: The environment children grow up in will shape who they become and who their children become.

Think about the child who grows up in the home described in this passage. The impact of that atmosphere will be profound. What the Israelite parents would do by conscious, consistent decisions, their children would tend to do automatically, out of habit. The same principle holds true today. We are powerfully shaped by our family histories.

But does God blame our parents for problems we have as adults? Should we hold our parents responsible for many of these problems? In the Bible we find two apparently contradictory principles regarding the impact of family backgrounds.

Deuteronomy 5:9 states: "You shall not worship [idols] or serve them; for I, the LORD your God, am a jealous God, visiting the iniquity of the fathers on the children, and on the third and the fourth generations of those who hate Me." Exodus 34:6–7 relates a similar message:

Then the LORD passed by in front of him and proclaimed, "The LORD, the LORD God, compassionate and gracious, slow to anger, and abounding in lovingkindness and truth; who keeps lovingkindness for thousands, who forgives iniquity, transgression and sin; yet He will by no means leave the guilty unpunished, visiting the iniquity of the fathers on the children and on the grandchildren to the third and fourth generations."

Is God unjust? Is he saying here that he will take revenge on the son because of sinful choices made by the father? Keep reading. In Deuteronomy 24:16 he states, "Fathers shall not be put to death for their sons, nor shall sons be put to death for their fathers; everyone shall be put to death for his own sin." In Ezekiel 18:20–21, God says this:

The person who sins will die. The son will not bear the punishment for the father's iniquity, nor will the father bear the punishment for the son's iniquity; the righteousness of the righteous will be upon himself and the wickedness of the wicked will be upon himself. But if the wicked man turns from all his sins which he has committed and observes all my statutes and practices justice and righteousness, he shall surely live; he shall not die.

The point of these passages is that God in his mercy does not punish us because of our parents' ungodly choices, but in his justice, God will allow the *consequences* of our parents' choices to affect us. Does that sound contradictory? I don't believe it is. Think about this: If the son of an idolater rejects idolatry and worships Jehovah, will God reward and bless that individual? Of course he will. Biblical examples include King Hezekiah, whose father was the wicked King Ahaz (2 Chronicles 29–32) and the godly King Josiah, whose father, King Amon, was ungodly (2 Kings 22–23). Both were blessed because of their own decisions, despite their fathers' idolatry and wickedness.

Yet the family that worships idols tends to raise idol worshipers, and idol worshipers will be punished. In this way, God allows the consequences of parents' sin to impact future generations because of our tendency to repeat familiar patterns.

Scripturally, it is clear that both principles are true. We are deeply affected by the patterns set by our parents, both godly and ungodly. But God assures us that we can be freed from sinful bondage by loving obedience and submission to him. We can choose new patterns of response that are not repetitions of our earthly parents' patterns but are responses to our heavenly Father. Understanding and changing these patterns is the theme and goal of *Your Family Voyage.*

Embarking on Your Family Voyage

As you sort through your family's past, look closely at individuals, situations, problems, victories, and crises, and numerous aspects of your own personality will be illuminated. Many of these discoveries may surprise you. Some will be exciting, positive strengths that you have never developed. Others will be stumbling blocks and false assumptions that need to be relinquished.

On this adventure you will learn to answer significant and profound questions you never before thought to ask. You will learn why you think and feel in a certain manner and come to understand why you act and react in ways that have been confusing to you and to those around you. You will gain insights into your parents, spouse, and loved ones. With these insights as a foundation, you will learn to make desirable changes in yourself and your relationships.

You may also find that your spiritual life has been impacted by your past. Your view of God, as well as your emotional reaction to spiritual issues, will be explored as part of your journey. Many people have found that as their past is clarified, spiritual insight deepens and broadens.

As you sort through your past, you will gain insight into your own choices, roles, relationships, and emotional reactions. You may discover that many of the struggles you have had really don't belong to you at all but are "baggage" from other family members. You may discover that many family superstars are far more fallible than the family history has portrayed them and some family villains are not villains at all. Some reactions and feelings that have been confusing to you will begin to make sense. You may or may not decide to discard them. As a result of this process you will be in a better position to help heal fractured relationships and get rid of "ghosts" that may have been causing problems for years. Along the way you will meet and get to know many people very well. Some of these people you've known all your life—some will be brand new acquaintances. One of them will be you.

Any significant voyage requires preparation. Before we set out on ours, there are a few more preliminary points that need to be understood. In our next chapter we will examine these prior to embarking.

Your Personal Family Voyage

1. If you could go back in time to your childhood and make a change in one person in your family, what would that change be? How would that change have affected your own development? How would that change have affected the development of other family members?

2. How was anger expressed or handled in your family of origin? In what ways was affection expressed by each of your parents?

3. In what ways are your own expressions of anger and affection similar to those of your family? How are they different?

For Those Who Are Married:

4. Which member of your spouse's family are you most similar to in each of the following:
   Your approach to conflict?
   Your expression of affection?
   Your expression of anger?

5. In what ways do you and your spouse promote childhood behavior in one another?

2

Foundational Family Principles

The lessons
we learned as children
within the family
we now apply to the world
outside the family.

J ack never saw his mother and father argue. Believing that conflict between them would cause insecurity in their children,
Jack's parents expressed any disagreements behind closed doors.
As a result, the children observed a relationship in which tension apparently didn't exist.

Now at thirty-three, Jack is single and almost desperate in his
longing for a loving marriage relationship. Yet his relationships are
consistently disappointing and always seem to follow the same pattern. Whenever he begins dating a woman, they develop a relationship that deepens for about six months. At that point some
disagreement arises between them, and Jack becomes extremely
anxious. Assuming that such incompatibility indicates a poor relationship, he finds all sorts of negative traits in that particular woman
and becomes disenchanted with her.

Jack's parents had a fine marriage: They were good role models
of affection and harmony. But Jack never had the opportunity to
observe them resolve conflict. Because of this, Jack developed a
belief that conflict could not be a part of a loving, satisfying, healthy
relationship. With idealistic and unreasonable expectations for relationships, he is one lonely man.

Hank's parents had grown up in poor families, struggling for the
necessities of life. Through determination and hard work, Hank's
parents significantly improved their financial situation and enjoyed
a middle-class lifestyle. They married later in life, and were both in
their late thirties when their son was born.

These caring people took pride in being able to provide more for
their son than they had received as children. Hank was the primary
object of their love, which they expressed in tangible ways such as
giving him gifts and doing him special favors.

As a child, Hank was the envy of his peer group. He had few responsibilities, a generous allowance, and the latest of whatever was popular. His relationship with Mom and Dad was good, as was communication. Hank felt loved and cared for.

Now as an adult, Hank struggles constantly with motivation. His interests are few and temporary; he is downright bored. Hank is known by all his friends as a procrastinator. His job performance reviews are consistently poor. Speaking directly to Hank, one boss described his attitude perfectly: "It's as if you're waiting for someone to do your job for you."

Susan's father had always been emotionally detached and distant. When she was young, Susan loved and admired her dad. She wanted nothing more than to spend time with him and have his undivided attention. Dad's passivity and uninvolvement never changed, however, and eventually Susan gave up any attempts to gain her father's affection.

You can probably guess what sort of men she found herself attracted to as a young adult. Inevitably they were passive, distant, and unexpressive. Susan seemed to have a hidden agenda in her relationships; she needed to change these men and somehow earn the affection she had never received from her father.

Going Home Again

The migration of salmon is a fascinating process. These fish hatch in freshwater streams high in the mountains, migrate amazing distances downstream to the ocean, and live the majority of their lives in salt water. Then, although they live for years in this foreign environment, they swim back upriver to the very pond, stream, or inlet where they were hatched years before. These fish have a powerful instinct to return to the familiar environment of their past.

Humans have a similar instinct. Our destination isn't geographical, however—it's emotional. We will naturally and consistently return to the emotional environment of our childhood. In many amazing ways we attempt to go home again emotionally by recreating the familiar setting of our childhood. We do this unintentionally and unconsciously, but we all do it.

We've all heard someone say, "I will never be like my dad!" or "When I get married, things will be different!" But are they? Typically we find that our adulthood experience is an extension of the patterns from our past. This tends to be especially true in areas we consider negative or problematic.

Not only do we repeat the patterns ourselves, but we elicit the help of others in keeping old habits alive. Regardless of whether we are aware of it, there is something mysteriously familiar about the people with whom we fall in love. Although it's usually unintentional, we are emotionally attracted to partners who complement or "fit" our family patterns. These are people who can help us maintain our family-of-origin roles.

The classic illustration of this is the young man in love. To his sweetheart during courtship he whispers, "I feel like I've always known you" and "It's like you're a part of me." Following the wedding he communicates the same message, albeit somewhat differently. Now he says, "You're just like my mother!" Same message, two approaches.

The human personality is extremely complex, which explains why volumes have been written about what makes us "tick." While I have no intention of oversimplifying these complexities, a basic understanding of several general principles will help you uncover and recognize your "finds." These principles will allow you to make sense of a number of very confusing pictures, memories, and situations that you will discover. Learn these principles and they will serve you well.

The Family Is Your Context in Adulthood

Mike cannot remember ever feeling good about his childhood family. As an adult, he had tried to avoid thinking about his past at all. The memories were not particularly enjoyable, and he had left them behind when he moved out at eighteen. Mike attempted to avoid the fact that we all carry our histories with us whether we want to or not.

Mike has no conscious memory of his father, who was killed in an auto accident just before Mike's second birthday. The grief of widowhood and the stress of single parenting apparently were overwhelming for Mike's mother; she left him at age four for his grandparents to raise. From that point on his contact with her was limited to an occasional visit every few years.

Life on his grandparents' farm was pleasant, but Mike felt emotionally detached from his grandparents. Parenting was difficult for this older couple, and Mike's needs were typically not addressed beyond the basic level of food, clothing, and shelter.

When Mike was ten, his grandmother died unexpectedly of a stroke. From that point on, Mike was largely cared for by two unmarried aunts. Each woman would stay at the farm for two to three weeks at a time, then return to town while her sister came to care for Mike and his grandfather, who suffered from severe and progressive arthritis. This pattern continued until Mike left home to join the Navy.

As an adult Mike was extremely frustrated by his relationships with women, which tended to be short-term and superficial. At twenty-eight, he desperately wanted a close, intimate relationship. Each of his previous relationships had ended with the woman leaving him because she needed "more space." Mike had become an insecure and emotionally dependent man whose demands for nurturance smothered his partners.

When Mike first came to my office, he was beginning a relationship that he valued highly. He had met Donna in church and admired her a great deal. After a few dates, they expressed a mutual interest in a deeper relationship. Knowing his tendency was to sabotage close relationships, Mike was determined to understand and change this pattern in his life.

In therapy, Mike sorted through his own history. He explored life on the farm, his relationships with the significant adults of his childhood, and some of the emotional baggage he had acquired growing up. Mike discovered that, although he had been cared for by some very good people, he had never really been loved. Mike's childhood had been one of function, not closeness—people had related to him out of duty, not desire. He had developed a subtle belief that only his neediness would keep people in his life. As an adult he knew intellectually that this belief was untrue, but emotionally, he lived out this assumption in every relationship.

Mike came to understand that the women of his childhood—mother, grandmother, aunts—had determined which of his needs would be met. These were people who were just out of reach emotionally and who were never in his life long enough for him to get close to them. They were also the ones who had left him.

Mike also discovered that he had learned to view men in general as weak, vulnerable, and needy. He viewed his father, grandfather, and himself as helpless victims of circumstance. For Mike, this perspective became a self-fulfilling prophecy in adulthood. He passively relinquished leadership in relationships and avoided all assertiveness out of his fear of rejection. As a result events constantly happened "to" Mike, and life seemed out of control.

Becoming aware of these assumptions and patterns was the first step for Mike. Once he had become aware of them, he realized they were key to his problems with relationships. This discovery gave Mike hope that change was possible.

Changing his relational patterns was the next step. As a child he had had no control over his circumstances; as an adult he did. The changes he desired would require that he make uncomfortable decisions. Since his emotions were so strongly influenced by his past, his relationships would have to be directed by what he knew and valued rather than by what he felt.

Both Mike and Donna valued their relationship enough to work on these issues together. Eventually Donna joined Mike in counseling, and as a couple they developed new ways of interacting. Mike learned to identify and communicate his emotions honestly and to keep them from controlling the relationship. Donna learned to identify ways in which she fed Mike's insecurity by communicating distance and distrust. Together they learned how to effectively affirm each other and their relationship. Slowly the patterns of Mike's past were replaced with security as well as open, genuine communication.

Your family is your beginning—your initial point of social involvement. For some, "family" means the traditional nuclear family of father, mother, and siblings. Others have grown up in single-parent households or in families with a stepparent and stepsiblings. Some may have been raised in an orphanage or other institution. Regardless of its specific form, your childhood family gives you a context or frame of reference through which you interpret your life experience. It was here that you first learned to perceive, react, communicate, trust, evaluate, and interact with others and where you learned who you were in relationship to the world around you.

Every family has consistent, yet almost imperceptible patterns of perceiving and doing things. Examples include the unspoken rules the family lives by, the emotional roles played by the various family members, and beliefs concerning anger and affection, pain and pleasure, and weakness and strength. All are communicated daily in hundreds of ways. To some degree your family of origin did not reflect how society in general operates. These differences may be as severe as violent brawls or as subtle as giving hugs to new acquaintances. To the degree that your family was a distortion of the rest of the world, your perceptions tended to be distorted as you entered adulthood. A child who grows up with chronic conflict, emotionally unavailable parents, or ridicule from family members will develop perceptions about himself or herself and the world based on these experiences. This is why family patterns of alcoholism, abuse, or other dysfunctions are so devastating to a child's development. They create a distortion in the family's experience of reality, to which the child adapts. The unresolved tension, unspoken fears, or chronic chaos becomes the "normal" experience of the child. These lessons learned subtly as children are often integrated into patterns of perception and reaction in adulthood.

It is difficult—some would say impossible—to understand much about an individual without knowing his or her context—that is, "where he's coming from." Your family of origin is a major factor in that context. When you were a child your family served as your whole world because it was all you knew. In childhood you learned to adapt and "fit into" that world. Family behavior was your teacher. You learned to "read" Dad and Mom. You learned what to do and what not to do, what to say and what not to say. You learned what hurt and what felt good, what was safe and what was dangerous. You learned countless lessons about how the family worked and how to work the family. You then applied the knowledge you acquired within the family to the world outside it. This process of "generalizing" is very natural, and its impact is incredibly profound.

Principle 1

Your family of origin is your context. Patterns from your primary relationships in childhood form your frame of reference by which you interpret your experiences in adulthood.

Repetition of the Familiar

The word *familiar* comes from the root *family*. That fact doesn't surprise me when I see clients such as Chuck and Cindy, who had been married for seven years when they came to me for counseling. They were committed to their marriage and loved each other but were deeply frustrated. Predictably, two or three times a month they would argue, and the conflict always seemed to follow the same pattern. Usually it would begin with Chuck complaining about something Cindy had or hadn't done that displeased him. Cindy would withdraw into silence, and Chuck would continue to press his point until Cindy would blow up and complain about a long list of offenses he had committed against her. He would accuse her of shifting the blame and avoiding the issue. She would accuse him of not listening to her and not caring. She would shout; he would shout; both would threaten to leave. This would continue until both were exhausted.

When they first came to my office, both Chuck and Cindy were discouraged and felt hopeless. They wanted to work things out but didn't see any way to break the pattern. They were seriously considering a divorce, even though neither really wanted one. During our first session together, the three of us made some interesting discoveries about their relationship.

Some questions about their family backgrounds revealed that Chuck had grown up in a home where verbal confrontation was standard fare. Yelling and expressing anger were considered natural outlets. As the eldest of four children, Chuck tended to lead the way in most things. Cindy, on the other hand, came from a home where angry words were taboo. She had no conscious memory of hearing her parents argue. She could clearly remember being sent to her room for expressing anger. Being an only child, she identified strongly with her parents and worked hard to please them.

Given these clues, we can see that Chuck and Cindy grew up with very different experiences of what love was and how it was communicated. Though neither family was necessarily right or wrong, Chuck and Cindy had very little common ground for expressing strong emotions.

In Chuck's home, love meant being open and honest. It meant not hiding one's feelings. He learned that when someone is silent and emotionally distant it's because that person doesn't care about the other individual or their relationship. For Chuck, love meant resolving differences. Silence was very threatening to him, especially from someone he loved deeply.

In Cindy's home, love meant protection. It meant being careful not to hurt another person's feelings. Harsh and loud words were an expression of hate. For Cindy, love meant choosing to be silent rather than saying anything that might cause pain. The verbal expression of anger was very threatening to Cindy, especially from someone she loved deeply.

Because of the differences in their backgrounds, Chuck and Cindy were set up to misunderstand each other and not notice that it was happening. An expression of love was actually interpreted as apathy or hatred because each partner's frame of reference was so different from the other's. The two were speaking completely different languages emotionally. Because those "languages" had developed so subtly over years of childhood, Chuck and Cindy were completely unaware of these differences. Both felt unloved and rejected, and both reacted accordingly.

Who was right and who was wrong was not the issue here. Much more important was their "differentness." For Chuck and Cindy, just learning to recognize their differences went a long way toward resolving their chronic conflicts. Once they understood the effects of the behavior patterns they had learned from their families of origin, they were better able to decide together what new patterns they would begin to establish. When they had made these decisions, they could begin to establish a style of conflict resolution different from either of their families.

Principle 2
In adulthood, your perceptions tend to be based on patterns that are familiar to you. These patterns were helpful to you at another time in your life and you have passively incorporated them through the years. In adulthood they may cause considerable difficulty.

The Impact of Emotional Memories

As long as she could remember, Dorothy had had a sense of anxiety and dread during the Christmas season. These feelings baffled her, as she could never recall a bad Christmas—she had only happy holiday memories from childhood. Nevertheless at age twenty-two, Christmas still caused Dorothy to want to escape and be alone. At times this anxiety reaction bordered on panic. These feelings significantly complicated her holiday experience.

Finally, a conversation with her parents and an aunt made some sense of this mysterious pattern. This particular conversation centered around her grandfather, who had died when she was four years old. She had never known that her parents had chosen to live in another state because Grandpa was an alcoholic, prone to drunken binges and violence. Direct contact with Grandpa was limited to his holiday visits—and during them the family "walked on eggshells" to keep from irritating him. Children were kept under tight control and periodically were hustled out of the house when Grandpa "began to brew." No one could recall if little Dorothy had ever actually witnessed one of Grandpa's explosions, as every effort had been made to avoid that occurrence.

Dorothy had no recollection of these events, no visual memory. Yet the tension that engulfed those early holiday experiences was deeply ingrained in her and affected her though she wasn't consciously aware of it. The discovery of this history was liberating. Dorothy could now see how normal, but unnecessary, her tension was. She now understood that her anxiety had served a purpose at one point of her life; it wasn't absurd or crazy. She could also see that it was no longer functional for her. This gave her the freedom to relax about it and let it go.

All of us have two forms of memory, each with its own specific function. One of these is our visual memory, a memory of pictures in our minds. Think of your fourth-grade teacher. Now think of the house you lived in in 1978. What you just did was flip through the "files" of your mind and pull out a picture of old Mrs. Magillicutty at her desk and a picture of the house on Elm Street. This form of memory—remembering—usually begins at around ages three to five and tends to fade in old age. It's concrete. We can readily say, "I remember that" or "I've forgotten."

We have a second form of memory, which isn't nearly so convenient as the first but is far more powerful and influential in shaping our lives. I call this second memory our "memory of sensations." You probably experienced it a moment ago when you brought out the picture of Mrs. Magillicutty. Whatever you felt when you viewed the picture in your mind was a sensation from the past. If your stomach got tight and you were cold and shaky, we could probably assume that your experience of that teacher had been one of fear and dread. If you felt warm and secure, it's probably because fourth grade with Mrs. Magillicutty was a positive experience for you. As soon as you recalled the visual image of this picture, the sensation was automatic. The two types of memory worked together for you, and you didn't even realize you had them!

Even though they work together, these two forms of memory are separate. Memory of sensation, more powerful than the visual memory, reaches further into your history and responds to details and situations that may have been lost to your visual memory. Dorothy "remembered" Grandpa's visits though she had no visual image associated with him. The lack of visual image may be because these particular images have been forgotten or blocked out, or perhaps they occurred before the visual memory was functional. Memories of sensations such as rejection, pain, abandonment, security, and excitement are all stored in this memory and can come out when it is "triggered."

Have you ever felt anxious about a place or situation and not known why? Have you ever disliked someone you just met without any particular reason? Have you ever felt attracted to someone and not understood why? These are probably times when the object of these mysterious emotions is associated with an emotional memory that has no corresponding visual memory.

Because of this memory of sensations, our present experience is made up of two components: our past experience and our current circumstances. These sensation memories are bound up with our families of origin. How we "fit," how we affected people, how that "world" operated—these gave us the foundations of who we are today. We built on those beginnings and they are still a part of us.

Principle 3
"Emotional memories," even with no conscious visual memory, often shape perceptions and behaviors.

Our personality "quirks" are certainly not always shaped by trauma or crises as were Dorothy's. More often we are molded by subtle but consistent patterns that influenced our formative years, as was the case for Chuck and for Cindy. As we progress on our voyage, watch carefully for such subtle, consistent patterns as well as individual experiences that may be impacting your life today.

With an understanding of these foundational principles, you are equipped to begin your exploration into your family history. Here is a list of other equipment that will be helpful to you. If you can't physically acquire these items, try to recall them in as much detail as possible. Enjoy your adventure.

1. Photo albums from your childhood and, if possible, from your parents' childhoods.
2. Letters, diaries, and other writings from family members.
3. Heirlooms, memorabilia, and other objects that have been preserved by a family member.
4. Anything else that may give information or impressions of life in your family of origin.

Your Personal Family Voyage

1. When you think of your own family of origin, what picture or image comes to mind most often? Describe the emotion you experience when these images come to mind. Are these emotions pleasant or unpleasant?

2. List five personality traits that describe your father.
   List five personality traits that describe your mother.
   Now ask a close friend or family member to list five personality traits that describe you. In what ways have you tried to avoid becoming like your parents?

3. How did your parents' spiritual attitudes affect you?

4. What were your parents' dreams or goals for your life? What is your dream or goal for your life? How do these goals differ? How are they alike?

5. In what ways are you dissatisfied with your life at this point?

6. What single character quality do you appreciate most in yourself? How has your family of origin contributed to the development of this quality?

For Those Who Are Married

7. How was your spouse's family of origin different from yours in the following:

   The expression of anger?

   The experience of affection and approval?

   The expectations placed on family members?

8. In what ways have these differences created tension in your marriage?

9. In what ways were your families similar?

10. What do you appreciate most about your spouse's family?

3

Who Is "We"?
The Family Identity

Deep within you
is a sense that you are a part
of a special group—your family.
As you define your family,
you tend to define yourself.

Your family of origin is unique: No other family is quite like yours. The peculiar combination of characteristics, personalities, experiences, and history that makes up your family has never been replicated anywhere. These distinctions give your family a personality all its own, a personality that is quite separate from those of its members. This "group personality" is what is known as the *family identity*.

You carry your family uniqueness with you like a fingerprint. As a result, you repeat patterns of behavior, not because they are necessary, positive, or even helpful, but simply because they are familiar. Because of this tendency, it's appropriate to begin your family voyage with this aspect of your family. Venturing into your family identity will deepen your understanding of who you are.

Our Deep Need for Belonging

It is important for families to feel special, so they develop many ways of both perceiving and expressing their uniqueness. Family members will make statements such as, "Davidsons have always been good in business"; "We Thomases love to socialize"; and "Church has always been important to the Nelsons." By identifying its unique traits, each family distinguishes itself from every other family and finds a distinctive place within society as a whole. Identifying similarities also gives members a sense of cohesion and togetherness—every family member identifies with special family qualities and therefore has a sense of belonging. Since each of us has this deep need for belonging, identifying our family as unique is a part of defining our own identity. Each family member identifies in some way with this unique family personality and as a result becomes part of something "special."

Most families enjoy finding distinctives and peculiarities that are unique to them. This seems to be true even if these qualities are not necessarily positive. Many families generate a sense of distinction from negative traits: "The James men have always locked horns with the law"; "We argue about everything; it's the Olson way of communicating"; "We hardly ever speak; that's how Schmidts get along."

Country singer Hank Williams Jr., expresses this well in a song entitled "Family Tradition." In it he explains some of his bad habits as a legacy from his family.

> I am very proud of my daddy's name,
> Although his kind of music and mine ain't exactly the same.
> Stop and think it over, put yourself in my position,
> If I get stoned and sing all night long, it's a family tradition.
>
> Lordy, I've loved some ladies, and I have loved Jim Beam.
> And they both tried to kill me in 1973.
> When my doctor asked me, "Son, how'd you get in this condition?"
> I said, "Hey Sawbones, I'm just carrying on an old family tradition."
>
> So don't ask me:
> Hank, why do you drink? Why do you roll smoke?
> Why must you live out the songs that you wrote?
> Stop and think it over, put yourself in my position,
> If I get stoned and sing all night long, it's a family tradition.[1]

Even an apparently negative identity builds a sense of togetherness, and it is certainly better than no identity at all because it can fulfill our need to belong. Generally, a family with no feeling of commonality will splinter and fall apart. Every family needs the cohesiveness that both comes from and is expressed by the family identity. This aspect of family life has a lot to do with how familiar patterns repeat themselves over the generations. The need we have for belonging gives each member a stake in the family unit.

1. Bocephus Music, Inc. BMI, c/o Dave Burgess Enterprises, P.O. Box 40929, Nashville, TN 37204. Used by permission.

Israel's Family Identity

Scripture is replete with examples of family identity. Abraham, Isaac, and Jacob and his twelve sons all carried the legacy of being God's chosen people. In this way, they identified themselves as being separate and distinct from those around them. Their lifestyles, goals, and attitudes reflected this common heritage.

The few boyhood years that Moses spent with his Hebrew family gave him a powerful sense of identification with them. Moses never lost his family identity as a Hebrew even after many years in Pharaoh's family. Forty additional years of living among foreigners did little to diminish this awareness of belonging. God used his family identification to change the course of history.

When God was directing Moses in the organization of Israel, he structured the Jews in family groups. In this marvelous way, God gave each Hebrew child a position that was unique. This structure also ingrained in them a sense of being a part of something bigger than themselves that was immeasurably significant.

Remember that God's plan for Israel was to bring his Messiah into the world. He was preparing a people through whom he would deliver salvation to all humanity. When establishing the nation of Israel, his chosen people, God gave them detailed instructions concerning virtually every facet of life. He also established a hierarchy of authority through the division of tribes and families. Through this structure as well as their history together, God gave the Israelites a sense of identity.

Why was God so picky and rigid in these details? I don't claim to know the mind of God, but I do know that he generally makes sense. In this case, God was leading his people into a land occupied by hostile nations with values and morals different from those of the Hebrews. They would be attacked, both militarily and ideologically, and many forces would attempt to tear the nation apart. God's law gave Israel stability, a sense of equilibrium in spite of the many changes taking place all around them. It served as a glue to unite them through their struggles.

Was it effective? Consider that the Jews were disobedient and rebellious. They were disciplined by God many times for their rejection of his direction. They were led into captivity and dispersed around the globe. They have been continually persecuted and slaughtered from the time of Pharaoh to the time of Hitler and even today in many places. They were without a homeland from A.D. 70 until 1948. But in spite of this, they have never lost their identity. Every other Old Testament nation in Canaan—the Jebusites, Philistines, Midianites—is completely gone, absorbed into other cultures and nations, even though in Old Testament times, they were more developed and sophisticated than Israel.

In Genesis 49 Jacob, on his deathbed, calls each of his twelve sons and blesses them. Jacob's pronouncements are both a reflection and an establishment of their identity and separate families. In the New Testament, nearly fifty generations later, and after enduring captivity, enslavement, persecution, and dispersion, the Hebrews still identify strongly with these twelve families. The individual Jew was still identified with the tribe of his forefathers. The importance of family identity is demonstrated throughout God's dealings with his people.

Family Rituals

Families build their sense of identity by repeating patterns of group behavior. We call these patterns *family rituals*.

"No one leaves the house without hugging everyone who's home."
"Dad fixes breakfast every Saturday."
"We visit the family grave every Sunday."
"Monday night we watch football."

Family rituals are unique to a particular family and are carried on without any significant notice. We become so accustomed to them that we are often unaware of their existence. Usually they are most apparent to us when they are missing or change in some way. One man told me that his mother had read *The Little Prince* to him every Christmas. As a child, especially while in junior high school, he hated the story and resented having to listen to it. He would pout and snicker and generally give his mother a hard time every time it was read. Nevertheless, on his daughter's first Christmas, he felt compelled to buy the book and read it to her. To his surprise, for him as a father, those memories held a warmth and fondness. The ritual of *The Little Prince* was an intricate part of his family Christmas.

During adolescence, when they begin to separate from the family and develop a personal identity, children generally begin to resist family rituals. Questioning, complaining, and challenging the way the family does things is typical of most teens. In this way, response to family rituals can be a measurement of how family members are feeling about themselves and how they relate to the family identity. A teenager who suddenly refuses to participate in family rituals or traditions may be expressing a need for autonomy or a fear of dependence on parents.

The family's reaction to the teenager's resistance may demonstrate the family's openness to change and differences among members. Some families find it easy to allow a growing teen the freedom to change or vary his or her role in family rituals. This may indicate the family's ability to allow the child to mature and separate from the family emotionally. Some families have extreme difficulty allowing adolescents to alter their part in family activities. Rigid adherence to specific rituals regardless of a child's needs or feelings may indicate a parent's fear of separation or a desire to keep a child dependent.

Divorce and Family Identity

When a divorce occurs it affects the family identity, of course. Some family members may refuse to let go of family rituals, while others may avoid mentioning previous family personality traits. Usually, as the family structure changes and stabilizes, a new family identity will emerge. Whether this transition is positive or negative depends on the responses of individual family members.

The loss of the family unit is a major casualty for everyone involved. It results in grief and the associated feelings of anger, sadness, failure, and shame. Families who avoid or forbid discussion of the loss of the family identity will see powerful emotions acted out in other ways. The result may be a disruption in the development of a new family personality. The new family identity may even be primarily negative as a result, and be expressed in statements such as "We are the family with the wicked stepmother" or "We're the kids who always run away from home."

Blending families through remarriage is an extremely difficult task. Part of this difficulty stems from several family identities being merged in an attempt to form a new family. When divorces and remarriages are repeated or perpetual within a family, these behavior patterns become very complex. The family personality becomes more difficult to identify, or it may form around the instability of divorce. The result is often insecurity in the children, who have no clear identification with a larger group.

Remembering Our Family Stories

A common family ritual is reciting family stories from the past. Every family seems to have a handful of tales that are retold regularly regardless of how often they've been heard before. Often the retelling occurs when some other family pattern or tradition is occurring, such as a holiday visit or family gathering.

"During the depression Grandpa used to . . ."
"Remember when Luke was a baby and he . . . ?"
"I'll never forget the time . . ."

Typically, the stories aren't new. They've been told dozens of times, often with the identical wording. After being heard so many times, they are not particularly surprising or even interesting. But most family members seem to enjoy hearing and telling them anyway, because they enhance family members' sense of identification with the group. These anecdotes affirm family membership through shared history and remind family members that they are connected with one another and are separate from those outside. They are special.

The perpetual retelling of these stories not only enhances a feeling of family unity, but also clarifies the family personality. Each account carries with it a piece of who you are. Each tale deals with something the family is proud of or enjoys doing together. It strengthens the family's self-esteem and usually builds the esteem of each member in some way.

Before you read any further, take a few minutes to recall several familiar stories from your family and make brief notes to ponder more deeply later. As you think about these stories, look for characteristics that tie the various stories together.

> Which memories are recounted most often?
> In what setting are they recited?
> Who usually tells which story?
> What feelings are generated by each story?
> How do various family members respond to each story?

The responses to these questions will serve as clues to your family's personality.

Emotional Family Boundaries

Tightly wrapped up in a family's personality is the concept of emotional boundaries. There are two types of emotional boundaries: personal boundaries and family boundaries. In this chapter we will explore family boundaries; we'll venture into the area of personal boundaries in chapter 8.

Emotional boundaries are similar to physical boundaries in many ways. An example of a physical boundary is a fence. A fence is built around a property line to control who has access to the property. Some fences are small and easy to step over; some are high, solid, and impassable. Some fences are in disrepair with sections missing, and it's difficult to tell where the property line is. Some fences have large gates that are always open, allowing people to enter and leave freely. Some fences have no gates, making it very difficult to enter and just as difficult to leave. Fences and emotional boundaries serve similar purposes. A family's emotional boundaries affect the way that particular family views and responds to people outside the family system.

Rigid family boundaries describe a situation in which a family has a low tolerance for and limited contact with non-family members. The Marluccis are a good example of a family with rigid boundaries. Since members are very close to each other, they almost never socialize outside of their extended family of uncles, aunts, and cousins. Their rigid boundaries are most evident when a family member gets married. Weddings are a time of great turmoil and conflict, and all the in-laws will tell you that they've never felt accepted by the family. Divorces are very common among the Marluccis.

Rigid boundaries may also be seen where a family has strict rules regarding topics of discussion with nonmembers. "Don't ever tell anyone what we talk about at home" is a message resulting from rigid family boundaries. A family with rigid boundaries discourages children from building relationships with outsiders. While rigid family boundaries may foster closeness and unity among family members, they also promote suspicion and distrust of outsiders. The shared message is "It's us against the world."

Weak boundaries are demonstrated by families who seem to be without a sense of who is family and who isn't. The Washburn family had weak boundaries. After the parents divorced, Dad moved to another state and was never heard from again. Subsequently, Mom had numerous boyfriends who would live with the family for awhile and then move out. During the kids' adolescence, an extra teenager always seemed to be staying with them. Just as often the kids would sleep over somewhere else. As the children grew up and left home, contact among family members disintegrated, and eventually they lost track of one another.

Weak boundaries both reflect and foster a sense of insecurity and unpredictability within the family. This often results in family members experiencing self-doubt and may be projected onto other relationships. Ambiguity, uncertainty, indecision, and isolation are common reactions to a history of weak family boundaries.

Flexible is the term used to describe a balance between these two extremes. Flexible family boundaries allow external input within clearly defined limits. There are recognized limitations to the influence outsiders may have over family functioning. Within the family, members' needs are prioritized above those of outsiders, who still receive utmost respect. The family allows itself to impact and be impacted by the people around it without compromising family values.

A Walk through Your House

Many insights about family personality can be uncovered by simply strolling through your childhood home in your memory. Every room is loaded with potential discoveries, subtly displayed through decor, arrangement, and function. The family dwelling communicates the family image and identity, both to outsiders and to the family members themselves. Decorations and furnishings can speak volumes regarding a family's view of itself, as well as how it wants others to perceive it. So, allow your memory to take a walk through the house. Remember that any evidences gathered here are only small parts of a bigger picture. The inferences I draw as we visit each room are only suggestions. Don't assume they are correct, but don't dismiss them immediately either. Consider them and look for other clues along the journey that may point you in a similar direction. You may discover a side of your family, and even yourself, that you never realized existed.

Before you go into the house, look around the yard. What condition is it in? Is it primarily trampled down and overrun with toys, or is it immaculately trimmed without a weed in sight? Each of these may indicate the family's priorities. Is the yard kept for children or for grown-ups, for visitors to see or for the family to use? How does this yard compare to others in the neighborhood? Is it the neatest or the most unkempt? The uniqueness displayed by either of these extremes may tell you that the family views itself as different from the neighbors in some way.

What happens as you enter the house? Many families have a rule against wearing shoes inside. This custom may indicate a desire to keep the outside world separate from the family. If the rule is just against wearing shoes in the living room, it may indicate a desire to present an idealized image and to look good to visitors. In either case this rule may reflect many other family secrets kept from outsiders.

As you glance around the house, note its condition. Does it look comfortably lived-in, run-down, or spotless? A house that is clearly neglected may indicate that relationships are neglected also. An immaculately clean house may indicate a good housekeeper or a cooperative family. It may also reflect intolerance of flaws or imperfection within the family unit. In some homes, family members constantly apologize to outsiders about the housekeeping; they are communicating that their expectations are for the house to be immaculate, even if it never is. This may be a signal of discontentment and dissatisfaction with life in general.

Many families set aside one room just for company. This room is "restricted space," kept especially clean, carefully decorated, and off limits to play. In such a case, make a note of the differences between this room and the rest of the house. The discrepancy is an indication of the value a family places upon the opinion of others. A significant difference between the visitor space and the family space is a reflection of a double standard, a need to present an image of a family that is different from the one that actually lives beyond the front room.

Do some furnishings have restricted usage? Maybe it's Dad's overstuffed chair or Mom's rocker ? These will often indicate who has power and control within the family, especially if the use is strictly enforced.

A houseful of antiques is typically reflective of a family seeking and valuing security, stability, and predictability. It may also express a desire to hold on to the past and discomfort with change. This is especially true if the antiques are family heirlooms. This same characteristic may surface as conflicts with in-laws or between generations where new, separate families have formed. If a family is uncomfortable with change in general, it will probably be most evident as "outsiders" enter the family and require changes.

A family room with furnishings arranged so as to focus toward the TV or a window may be communicating discomfort with close, personal interaction. When family members have difficulty with emotional closeness and intimacy, the focus of attention becomes some other, "safer" object or issue such as television, job, neighbors, or the weather.

The living room or parlor where guests spend most of their time communicates many unspoken messages and expectations. Family portraits and photos found only in the living room and nowhere else send a message about the family's image. The message is primarily directed to outsiders: "We are an attractive, happy family." Placing many books on prominent display may be a family's way of saying, "We are smart and that's important to us." The specific titles even communicate specific messages about the family identity. Prominent shelves that house primarily theology books say, "We are spiritual." Psychology and self-help books say, "We are well adjusted and self-aware."

Children's rooms that clearly have been designed by parents tell much about the parents' attitudes toward and expectations for their children. The parents' ability to allow responsibility, expression of emotions, and imperfection, all are reflected in what can be tolerated in a child's room. When a child's room is clearly decorated and maintained by a parent, that parent may be unable to allow the child to express independence and individuality. The treatment and condition of a child's room communicate a family's expectations regarding performance and imperfection and indicate whether the child is given privacy and responsibility or is overprotected. Of course, the age of the child should be considered before drawing conclusions. A twelve-year-old is capable of maintaining a bedroom in a much different fashion than a two-year-old.

The bathroom is an interesting place to explore because it is the room where people do private things. Almost every family's bathroom contains basically the same equipment and supplies. How these sundries are treated tells something about the family's expectations for privacy. Is the bathroom in your childhood home a showplace? Are all toiletries and grooming paraphernalia carefully hidden from view as though they don't exist, or are they strewn about with caps off and labels missing? Perhaps your home had more than one bathroom. Was one set aside only for use by company? If so, what message does it convey to outsiders about the use of this private room?

As you continue your stroll through the house, be sure to peek into each room—kitchen, family room, bedrooms, den. You may find it helpful to draw the floor plan of the house as you remember it. Pay attention to the details in each room. It's a pleasant way to spend some time and may unveil fascinating insights about the family.

When you've completed your walk through the house, take another step forward by personalizing some of these memories. Place yourself as a child in that house and recall what it was like to live there.

Which room was your favorite?

What fond memories do you relate to that room?

With which rooms are your clearest and strongest memories associated?

Does any particular part of the house carry with it negative or painful memories?

Do you associate certain family members with specific rooms? Why?

What do these various memories indicate to you regarding your own sense of family identity?

Anxiety Attacks and Family Patterns

Thirty-three-year-old Sharon came to my office following a number of increasingly severe anxiety attacks, during which she experienced shortness of breath, accelerated heart rate, and feelings of panic. Afraid she was developing a serious illness, she initially went to her family doctor and received a thorough physical checkup. He assured her that she was in fine health and referred her to me.

Even after her doctor's assessment and recommendation, it took three months and four additional panic attacks before Sharon called for an appointment. Months later she admitted the reluctance, embarrassment, and shame she felt at the prospect of discussing personal problems with a stranger.

Nothing in Sharon's immediate situation seemed especially extreme. She had been married four and a half years to her husband, Stan. They had a two-and-a-half-year-old daughter, Stephanie, and considered their marriage and family happy. Sharon said that tension had recently increased in their marriage because Stan had changed jobs six months earlier. She was concerned that Stan might want her to find a job to supplement his income—a situation Sharon said would look bad to their family and friends. She also expressed frustration with Stephanie's increasing independence, or rebellion, as Sharon called it. Sharon considered neither of these stressors extreme, though she had no close friends with whom she felt comfortable discussing them.

After several sessions, Sharon began to relax in therapy. She started opening up and exploring her own feelings, something she couldn't remember having done before. She shared feelings of anger toward her daughter, which brought an immediate response of guilt and shame. She talked about things her husband was doing that were increasingly irritating. Several decisions he had made had hurt her but discussing these issues with Stan seemed impossible to Sharon.

These normal tensions of family life left Sharon feeling overwhelmed. As the stresses of marriage increased with neither resolution nor outlet, her feelings deepened into a persistent sense of dread and occasional panic. Emotionally she was suffocating.

Sharon reluctantly agreed to spend several sessions exploring her family of origin. She was quick to assert that her parents had been good to her and that her problems were not their fault. I assured her that sorting through the family baggage is not a witch hunt. It is merely a way of examining our personal history to gain an understanding of the various perceptions and reactions each of us develop. Despite her foreboding sense of disloyalty, Sharon decided to begin.

As she explored her family history, Sharon affirmed her childhood as generally a happy time. She felt loved and cared for, she suffered no physical or sexual abuse, and for the most part, she respected her parents. She and both her brothers, one older and one younger, had had very few conflicts while growing up. In spite of this exceptional harmony, there remained little closeness among them today. Though none reflected hostility, their contact was limited to an occasional holiday visit.

Sharon's father was a man of great self-control who demonstrated little emotion. He had been a pastor in a conservative denomination, as were both of her grandfathers. Her mother was a stern woman, committed to supporting her husband wherever he felt God leading him. The result of this union was a family strongly determined to act correctly in every situation. Correctness was defined by a narrow set of behaviors and expectations traditional to conservative churches of the previous generation.

As is often the case, the pastor's family had many expectations placed on it by the congregation. This particular family, the Hawkinses, did a remarkable job of fulfilling those expectations. Pastor Hawkins's family had been the ideal representation of a Christian home. This family identity was accepted by all who knew them. As the "ideal family," they could not express anger, discuss conflict, or share strong opinions. Any opinions expressed were either followed by a passage of Scripture or dropped from discussion. Any complaint or expression of dissatisfaction was met with a Scripture quotation and an admonition to "be thankful in all things." Sharon could recall many lectures about others looking to them as an example and the need to live above reproach. As Sharon examined these memories, she became aware of growing up with a subtle sensation of being watched. It had seemed vaguely as though someone were following her.

While she couldn't remember any open conflict between her parents, Sharon recalled several times when they had exchanged sharp words. Each confrontation was followed by several days of oppressive silence. Sharon remembered being fearful during these times of tension. One such occasion occurred when Sharon was fourteen. Following her parents' long silence, Sharon mustered the courage to ask her father if they would ever divorce. Her father's reply was indirect and confusing to Sharon. He said, "There has never been a Hawkins divorce." End of discussion. No mention of love, commitment, forgiveness, or God's will. Only a statement of family tradition.

Her family identity became an interesting study for Sharon. She found that it required that any overt anger be avoided at all costs. Though it had never occurred to her, Sharon had grown up with the assumption that any emotional tension was wrong. Apparently the same was true for most other emotions. She had no memories of spontaneous laughter or playful humor. When her grandfather died, ten-year-old Sharon was reprimanded for her tears and admonished to rejoice since Grandpa was with the Lord. Repeated in numerous situations and in many subtle ways, the message Sharon received was that there was no room for negative feelings in family life.

Viewing the family as an adult, Sharon was surprised by the number of stress symptoms borne by family members: Dad had suffered from colitis for more than twenty years. Mom had a long history of severe migraine headaches. William, her thirty-five-year-old brother, had had an ulcer since adolescence. (He had left home at eighteen, moved across the country, and rarely contacted anyone in the family.) Thomas, her younger brother, was a very quiet man. In poor health generally, he shared his mother's pattern of regular migraines. While each family member suffered symptoms of emotional stress and repression, each of them unknowingly prioritized the family image above personal health. In this context, Sharon's anxiety attacks were no longer surprising.

Sharon made many discoveries on this journey. One revelation was her family's very clear and strongly accepted identity. The Hawkinses defined themselves as the family that did things correctly, no matter what. This identity required absolute harmony at all costs. Not only did Hawkinses not divorce, they did not argue, get angry, get depressed, or misbehave in any way. While the family image was a positive one, the impact on individuals was not.

As a result of her emotional journey, Sharon decided to initiate some changes. In spite of her feelings of apprehension, she shared with Stan her feelings of hurt over some of his responses and decisions. To her surprise, Stan didn't react defensively. In fact, he was grateful for her honesty. They were able to clarify several misunderstandings and reevaluate some of those decisions. Her successes in this relationship gave Sharon the courage to begin sharing her struggles with her two closest friends. They both welcomed the opportunity to deepen their friendship and responded by sharing similar struggles of their own.

Sharon's family had no villain. The negative patterns were the result of generations of unchallenged assumptions typical of that era. By unveiling the family identity of her childhood, Sharon was able to redefine herself apart from her family. She could choose personal values that were consistent with her spiritual convictions but separate from her family of origin. She could work through her feelings of shame and disloyalty as a reflection of her past, not as a current issue. As she grew and developed in these areas, her anxiety attacks subsided.

As you can see, your family identity is a powerful factor in who you become as an adult. It reveals a great deal about why you behave and react in certain ways. While it is certainly significant, it is only the first stage of identifying both the gems and garbage that are stored in your attic. Write down any new information you have acquired to this point. Remember to accept this information with some tentativeness. Add it to the information you gather as you proceed. In time you can begin to draw conclusions and decide which parts of your family history to accentuate and which to let go.

Your Personal Family Voyage

1. Read through the Appendix and draw a genogram of your family. Leave space to add information you uncover through your explorations.

2. In what ways was your own family of origin unique compared to other families you know?

3. Complete the following sentences regarding your family of origin.
   We were the family that . . .
   One thing we always did was . . .
   What we really enjoyed together was . . .
   I'm sure others would describe us as . . .

4. Describe the behavior patterns you see in each of your responses to question 3.

5. Would you consider these responses positive or negative?

6. In what ways do these statements describe you today?

7. What do you value most about your family identity?

For Those Who Are Married

8. Ask your spouse to complete the sentences regarding his or her family of origin in question 3. Compare your statements to those of your spouse's. How is your relationship affected by the differences? How have you personally grown from learning about your partner's family history?

9. How would you complete the sentences in question 3 regarding your current family?

10. What, if anything, would you like to change about your current family identity? In what way? How would you go about implementing a change?

4

"Places Everyone"
Roles within the Family

Each family drama requires
that many parts be played.
The plots may change and scripts may vary,
but roles tend to be remarkably consistent.
However insignificant a part may appear,
the plot is dependent on every role
being played on cue.

John and Mary Smith are the parents of three children: Megan, eighteen; Jim, sixteen; and Danny, eight. John is very successful as a traveling sales representative for a major corporation. Mary works part-time as a hairdresser. Though they all consider their family life to be happy, John and Mary's marriage has always been rocky. Mary blames John's drinking and traveling for the discord. John blames Mary's domineering attitude.

Very little overt tension is expressed in the Smith home. When tension between Mary and John begins to build, the family response is fairly predictable. As conflict surfaces, either Mary or John will make a seemingly casual remark to Megan. "Your mother is impossible," or maybe, "He is so blind." At this point Megan attempts to make peace by clarifying each parent's point of view. "What Dad means is . . ." or "You know Mom really . . ." are fairly standard lines. Soon the tension subsides.

Jim is seldom around when there is conflict. He has been very active in athletics since he was eleven, and at sixteen he is now the star quarterback on the school football team. The family is very supportive of Jim and never misses his games. Playing football professionally had been John's dream when he was younger. While his own dream never materialized, he is extremely proud of his son's potential. Of course, this commitment to athletics keeps Jim away from home quite a bit, but no one seems to mind. Much of the family's conversation is about Jim's games.

The family's nickname for Danny is "Scamp," and it fits him well. He is very active and sociable and has many friends. It seems that Danny is always in some sort of minor trouble, usually for some sort of practical joke or childish mischief. Though the consequences are never very severe and often fairly humorous, they are enough to require his parents' attention and concern. Mary and John seldom argue when Danny is being reprimanded. In fact, they often laugh together over his antics.

Do you recognize the Smiths? They are very typical and not terribly dysfunctional. Perhaps your family was or is much like them. Perhaps they are similar to many families you know.

Let's make a change in the Smith family. Let's say that Jim drops out of school or moves away from home. How would this affect the family? Dad would lose his vicarious sense of success. The family would lose a major source of positive conversation, its primary family activity, and its diversion from the parents' conflict and tension. We can assume that either tension would increase dramatically or another diversion would arise. My guess is that Danny would begin getting into more serious trouble. That way he would still get attention and his parents could still avoid resolving their own relationship problems. Of course, for Danny that would mean a role change from cute, youngest child to family troublemaker. I wonder if his nickname would change?

What do you suppose would happen if Megan suddenly were to decide to get married? Mom and Dad would lose their mediator; their arguments wouldn't conclude as quickly. Tension would escalate or another diversion would develop. I wouldn't be surprised if John started drinking more. Then he might take the role of family problem and everyone could blame him for any tension that exists.

The System: Parts Working as a Whole

Have you ever felt that your life is nothing more than an elaborate dramatic production? Sometimes the events of family life give that impression. In some ways families function as though their behavior is controlled and choreographed by some invisible director. That feeling can be in large part attributed to the fact that a family is a system.

While growing up in San Francisco I spent a great deal of time working in my father's printing shop. I was intrigued by the mechanical operation of the presses. Those presses are probably antiques by today's standards, but for me they were the ultimate in technology. Vast numbers of gears worked together to allow the press to function, with each gear serving its unique purpose. No single gear could be removed or changed in any way unless *all* of the other gears were altered to compensate for the loss. Otherwise the press would come to a screeching halt.

Those gears are a good example of what we call a *system*—a set of interdependent parts that make up a functioning whole. Anything that affects one part affects the whole system. Every system has a purpose. When something blocks movement toward that purpose, most systems will attempt to adapt in some way. Our world is full of systems, from the solar system to systems of government. Some systems are less apparent than others, but all function in similar ways.

A small midwestern town once sponsored a coyote hunt to reduce the number of animals killing the farmers' chickens. Fifteen hundred coyotes were killed in a weekend. Within a few months the community was overrun with rodents because their main predator had been eliminated. Within a year the rodents had become less of a problem because the rattlesnakes were everywhere. With much more food available for them, they had reproduced rapidly. At that point the chickens were safe, but the humans were in danger. The coyotes had been an important part of the environmental system, the food chain. When one part of the system changed, other parts adapted to the new reality.

The human body is a system. We can survive the loss of many of our body parts, but the remaining members will naturally change in some way to compensate. If you were to lose your sight, your other senses would become much more acute. Unless you're blind, it's difficult to imagine having fingers sensitive enough to read Braille. But the sense of touch develops to compensate for the loss of sight— the members of the system work together.

First Corinthians 12 describes the church as a system with each participant serving an essential purpose regardless of how insignificant it may seem. In verses 10–31 Paul explains that each member of the body of Christ has a distinct function, but all are interdependent. The message Paul gives is that we cannot minimize the value of anyone within the church, because we all affect one another in many ways.

The family is a system as well, a relational system whose purpose is to maintain stability among the members in spite of changes outside of the system. This is why family patterns tend to be so persistent and enduring. Yet there are negative, or dysfunctional, ways of maintaining stability within a family, such as when a child misbehaves whenever Mom and Dad argue, or a mother gets physically ill whenever the children plan to leave home. The individuals involved are usually unaware that their "problems" are serving the purpose of maintaining some semblance of family stability.

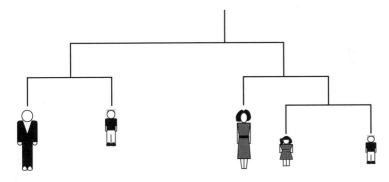

The family system is often diagrammed as a hanging mobile. On a mobile, each piece is carefully hung to balance in relation to the others. Each piece is connected to every other in some way. Some connections are very direct and clear; some are distant and complex. Because of these connections, every single "member" of the mobile is interrelated; none is independent of any of the others.

When all of the parts of the mobile are in balance, the mobile hangs quietly, serenely. If any part is adjusted or moved in any way, the entire mobile is thrown into a chaotic jumble of movement. This gradually slows down as each part adjusts in some way to the new balance. Eventually a new equilibrium is found. If a permanent change has been made to any one piece, the new equilibrium leaves every piece in a new position. If any individual piece of the mobile becomes stuck on something or immobilized in some way, the entire mobile begins to revolve around that one piece.

When a baby is born or a family member dies, or when someone graduates or drops out of school, the entire family adjusts. Some adjustments are subtle; others are more noticeable. Some adjustments cause problems; others are beneficial. Often they are responses to previous family adjustments.

As a relational system, the family will do everything in its power to maintain internal equilibrium in spite of external change. Think about family identity, which was discussed in the previous chapter. A family sees itself as "special" so the group will maintain stability. If there is a divorce in the family, after much shaking and chaos, a new family identity will emerge. At a later date blending families through remarriage may be just as traumatic, as two families—two delicate mobiles—become one and find a new equilibrium.

In this chapter we are going to look at informal family roles. For good and for bad, the roles serve one purpose: family stability. Sometimes the price paid for stability of the family is the emotional health of its members.

Casting the Roles

Each family drama requires that many parts be played. The plots may change and scripts may vary, but roles tend to be remarkably consistent. The story line in your own family may have been similar to "Leave It to Beaver," "Peyton Place," or "Gunsmoke." Whatever the plot, the script requires that every member be assigned a role, and sometimes several roles. However insignificant a part may appear, the plot is dependent upon every role being played on cue.

There are two types of family roles: *formal* and *informal*. *Formal* family roles have recognizable labels of mother, father, husband, wife, student, infant, and so forth. Our expectations for these roles are shaped by our culture and are fairly consistent. We all generally know what a father is, though every father is unique. The literature available on formal roles is almost endless. Volumes have been written on understanding and improving performance in each role.

Informal family roles are much less obvious than formal roles. Though they seem subtle, they have a profound effect on our emotional development. Informal roles revolve around emotional tasks that individuals carry out for the rest of the family. These may be performed consciously, but more often they are unconscious.

The general function of all informal family roles is to regulate tension—maintain stability—within the family. They may or may not be successful. Tension and conflict are natural parts of any relationship. Conflict in itself is not good or bad, right or wrong. In many ways it may be a sign of life, growth, and progress. An old saying is worth consideration: "If two people agree on everything, one of them isn't necessary." Although tension is normal, how that tension is handled will determine whether it is positive or negative. Too much conflict in a family will result in chaos; too little will result in stagnation. Informal roles are an attempt to regulate the tension—balance the mobile. Through family roles each of us learns how to respond to uncomfortable emotions such as anger, hurt, and sadness. In these roles we learn to deal with the feelings of others as well. Long before we reach adulthood, we have learned our roles so well that they seem instinctual. Most of us give them no thought at all. We say things like, "That's my personality" or "That's just the way I am." In reality, we are acting out what we learned we must be, at least at one point in life. Let's take a look at some specific roles to clarify what this means.

The Family Success

All her life, everyone liked Tina. Her outgoing personality and quick wit naturally attracted people. During her teens, Tina was the girl known for doing things well. She made excellent grades and excelled in athletics. She was popular, attractive, sharp. She even got along well with her moody, critical, impulsive father—something nobody else in the family did very well.

This was in contrast to her brother, who was an endless source of trials to their parents. His drug and alcohol abuse and clashes with the law made Tina's success shine more brightly by comparison. It was in the context of this family that Tina developed the subtle, though powerful, belief that her value and acceptability could only come from her ability to perform. Although Tina wasn't aware that she felt this way, it became evident in early adulthood.

Tina came to my office, desperately depressed. Besides an overwhelming sense of sadness, this twenty-three-year-old woman complained of sleeplessness, loss of appetite, lethargy, and emotional isolation. She said she had felt this way for some time and could see significant problems ahead if things didn't change soon. Her family doctor had recommended several sessions of counseling prior to prescribing medication for her depression.

Tina's depression had begun three months earlier when she had lost her job after a year of employment. This had been her first position following college and was a challenging job she enjoyed. Her boss had made it clear that the layoff happened because of budget cutbacks, but Tina was convinced that her performance had been the problem, since she was the only employee let go. Tina said she had been unable to look for another job due to her depression, which seemed to worsen with each passing day. Her thought patterns, while fairly typical in depression, were uncharacteristic of Tina: What if I can't find another job? I may never make it in the world of adults. No one really cares about me.

Her depression was complicated by the fact that Tina had no one with whom to share her fears and frustrations. Any mention of the situation to her family was met with either critical directives or passive avoidance. Tina was unwilling to share her struggle with any of her friends. She was sure none of them could handle her feelings because they had never seen anything like this in her. Through this bout with depression, Tina discovered how very superficial her relationships were. For Tina, people had been kept at a safe distance emotionally and now were not available for support.

Tina had maintained the role of family hero. Through most of her life she had avoided situations in which she would not excel. The loss of this job made it clear that this role would not function well outside the family. This was the first experience of failure in Tina's memory and it called for some changes.

Tina needed to learn to allow herself to fail. Her high expectations "set her up" for overreaction to unsuccessful experiences. She was very compassionate regarding failure in others, but she had very little tolerance for imperfection in herself.

More importantly, Tina needed to develop close, trusting relationships with friends with whom she could share such unsettling experiences and who would affirm her in the midst of these hardships.

These were risks Tina was willing to take. She already had a number of friends she felt were worthy of such trust, but until now she had never opened up to them emotionally. As she began to share some of her more sensitive and vulnerable issues, these people responded with similar openness, and the relationships deepened.

Tina recovered from her depression fairly quickly, and now she had the resources to avoid such an emotional downfall in the future.

Heroic Qualities

Every family needs a success story. The qualifications for this role may vary among families, but many families cast one member as the "family hero," or "good child"—the member the others would describe as the most successful. The task of this member is usually to represent the family in a positive light to outsiders. Family heroes come in all shapes and sizes, but some characteristics are fairly typical. This "good child" tends to be the ultraresponsible member who does things "correctly." This is often one of the older siblings who takes on parental responsibilities for the younger children. The terms *caring, considerate, competent,* and *dependable* are usually good descriptions for people in this role. While almost every family will have a member with a number of these positive traits, the characteristics will be more pronounced in families with dysfunctions. The more profound the dysfunction, the more pronounced the role. We see this role emerging most prominently in families where one or both parents are negligent. Alcoholism, abuse, and mental illness generally create emotional voids into which this member steps.

Family heroes grow up learning to fulfill the expectations placed on them, which for a variety of reasons have been high. They develop an acute sense of how they come across to others. Appearances are important to them. It is also very important for the good child to do the "right" thing in any situation. This gives this member the tendency to be fairly rigid, generally thinking, "To be right is good and to be wrong is bad, and it's terrible to be bad." This perspective on life can make an individual very controlled and very controlling. Heroes often find it difficult to relax and be spontaneous.

As children, family heroes do well in most situations; the skills involved in pleasing others are learned early in life and refined in many ways. Family heroes have a strong need to please authority figures and are generally pretty good at it. Heroes find many rewards in school. Most teachers enjoy having them in class, and with good reason. Not only do they do their work, but they also tend to be good examples to the rest of the class. Good grades and adult recognition provide ready reinforcement for their role. Most family heroes operate well within the traditional authority structures and tend to stay out of trouble. They mind their parents and teachers; they accomplish what is expected of them; they don't make many waves for the adults in their world. In return they are rewarded with positive feedback and approval based on their performance.

There are several variations on the role of family success, including the family hero, the lieutenant, and the rescuer.

The Family Hero

A child who is fairly independent of the family in his or her success—the athlete, scholar, or musician—is seen as the family hero. Success is measured by how he or she projects himself or herself to outsiders. This child's emotional bond to other family members is generally not as close as other "good children." Typically, this child's closest relationships are with people outside the family.

The Lieutenant

Another variation on the family success is the child who takes on some or all of the parental responsibilities for the siblings. This role of "lieutenant" may develop out of obedience to the directives from parents (having learned to take orders from above) or to fill a void left by irresponsible, negligent, preoccupied, or otherwise unavailable parents (having learned to take charge). This child's success is measured primarily by how he or she interacts within the family.

The Rescuer

A child who has taken over one particular aspect of parenting, that of nurturing—encouraging, supporting, and caring for siblings— becomes a "rescuer." Usually this is a job taken on because no one else was doing it. The negative side of this role is that someone else must have a problem or be in pain for the rescuer to function.

Adult Heroes

Family heroes tend to carry these traits into adulthood. Outwardly they are productive, hardworking, motivated, and self-controlled. They often live with a vague sense of guilt over what they cannot accomplish. Their strong need to please everyone leads to patterns of overcommitment and unrealistic expectations for themselves, which often result in unfulfilled commitments, half-completed tasks, or exhaustion. These in turn lead to more guilt. Family heroes experience failure as rejection. Often this rejection is self-inflicted, but it is painful just the same. Their response to rejection is to work harder, and that's just what they do. It is difficult for these overresponsible "children" to maintain a realistic assessment of their own capabilities. Most never had the chance to learn that they could fail and still be loved. Their sense of acceptance and belonging became dependent on good performance.

Heroes also tend to be difficult to get close to emotionally. They don't let their guards down very easily. Looking good means feeling good and vice versa. To become open and vulnerable to another person would mean admitting fears and shortcomings they hide even from themselves. For the family hero, the risks in relational transparency are high. Because of these patterns, these "good children" tend to be manipulated fairly easily. Frequently motivated by guilt and a fear of self-perceived failure, they invest a great deal of energy in the approval of others, often compromising their own convictions, values, and emotional needs to avoid the criticism they may receive by not fulfilling another person's expectations. The need for approval from authorities in childhood frequently develops into a "need to be needed" mentality in adulthood. People who fall into this pattern generally become rescuers—over-responsible people who tend to be attracted to under-responsible individuals who need their help. These roles tend to complement each other, fulfilling a number of emotional needs in each partner. The familiar roles repeat patterns from childhood and are somewhat comfortable, but the resulting relational patterns are seldom satisfying for the hero-rescuer. We will explore this relationship pattern further when we look at the next family role—the "scapegoat."

The Scapegoat

Carl was referred to my office by his pastor—the most recent of a long list of Carl's counselors, none of whom seemed to have been particularly helpful. Though the issues addressed in counseling had been many and varied, Carl's current struggle was regarding a broken relationship with a woman.

Carl was a very likable fellow—he was good-looking, articulate, and intelligent, though very discouraged and pessimistic. At twenty-eight, he often described his life as a total waste. His current depression was affecting his performance at work, which had been shaky to begin with. He reported having very few close friends and no support from or contact with his family.

As his story unfolded, I began to see that Carl had a way of sabotaging potential success in every area of his life. He had lost several promising jobs by repeatedly "forgetting" important responsibilities or simply not showing up for work. A number of supervisors had shown surprising patience with Carl's erratic performance but eventually had let him go. Carl never seemed to retain friendships beyond the level of superficial acquaintance. As a friendship deepened, Carl typically "smothered" his friend with demands for time and attention until an emotional distance resulted. Most friends had "burned out" on Carl.

On several occasions Carl had been in potentially meaningful and long-term relationships with women. In each case, after several months of positive experiences, he lost interest and neglected the friendship until the woman withdrew or went on to another relationship. Carl viewed the experiences as rejection and a reflection of the woman's unwillingness to pursue a relationship with him.

Carl entered therapy following one such broken relationship. Depressed and discouraged, he was convinced that his life was destined for grief and failure. He had a good deal of evidence to support that conclusion, but he wasn't considering the evidence of his past.

Carl was the firstborn son of Merle and Lucille. Carl and his brother, Merle Jr., had grown up in a small farming community in Iowa. He considered his childhood normal, though not particularly happy. Carl was in trouble for one thing or another during much of his youth and had several brushes with the law during adolescence. He remembered his father telling him that he was a loser and would never amount to anything, but Carl considered that simply his father's expression of anger and dismissed it as having no impact on him. Carl also recalled that his younger brother was virtually his opposite. Successful, compliant, and popular, Merle Jr. seemed to cruise through life with little struggle.

While exploring his family history, Carl had several extended conversations with older relatives and made a number of sig-

nificant discoveries. It was no secret within the family that Carl
had been conceived before Merle and Lucille were married. Carl
had been aware of this fact while growing up but had never given
it much thought. What had been kept secret, however, was that
Merle had always suspected that Carl had been conceived while
Merle was attending college in another state. Merle had married
Lucille under pressure and with deep resentments that had never
been resolved. The rockiness of the marriage was attributed to
this first child; Carl's very existence was both an embarrassment
and a painful reminder to his parents. Ideally a child's birth is
greeted with excitement and anticipation, but Carl's birth was
met with regret, resentment, and anger.

As he sorted through his history, Carl began to see how the
expectation of failure had been communicated to him in hundreds of ways throughout childhood. Had his patterns of avoiding success been a form of loyalty to his family? A light dawned.

These discoveries were by no means the resolution of Carl's
struggles. He had years of bad habits to break, and many relational skills to learn and practice. But knowledge and understanding gave Carl a new sense of self-determination. His life
pattern was a role that could be relearned and changed based on
decisions he could make. Familiar patterns, though comfortable,
were not his destiny.

The Scapegoat Role

The concept of a scapegoat comes from Leviticus 16:7–22. If
you've never read this passage, take a moment to do so now. It will
help to illuminate this particular family role. According to Jewish
law, the high priest was required to take a goat, which was chosen
by casting lots. This goat was taken before the people by the high
priest, who then placed his hands on the head of the goat and sym-
bolically transferred the sins of the Israelites onto the goat. The goat
was then led into the wilderness and released, destined to wander

aimlessly and alone in the desert until it died. The people of Israel were then free from the guilt of their sin because the scapegoat had borne the blame for the group.

Almost every dysfunctional family has a member who plays the role of family scapegoat. The more severe the family dysfunction, the more obvious the scapegoat role will be—especially to those outside the family. It is the scapegoat's job to bear the bulk of the blame for the family problems. In this way the scapegoat reduces tension in the family. Usually the scapegoat began the role by trying to succeed and please Mom and Dad, but for one reason or another was not able to do that. Perhaps an older or more gifted sibling in the role of hero made competition impossible. Perhaps the parents had unreasonable expectations and demands that promoted constant failure. Whatever the initial cause, the scapegoat learned to believe that recognition could be achieved only through negative means. Gradually this child began to believe that rejection and failure were a part of who he or she was. Like the Old Testament scapegoat, this family member is emotionally sent away and feels as if he or she is on the outside looking in on family life. These feelings of rejection are rarely verbalized. A small child may express these feelings by hiding under the bed or in a far corner of the house. A teen may become involved with peers who share similar frustrations and offer the affirmation he craves. Alcohol or drug abuse is especially common if one or both parents have chosen the same route of escape from pressure or tension.

Generally the scapegoat isn't consciously aware that he or she is choosing this role, which can be very subtle in its evolution. Though not conscious of the role, scapegoats have an uncanny way of directing blame toward themselves. At times they may even create situations in which they can be blamed in order to minimize tension in the rest of the family. Every member needs to achieve a feeling of belonging in the family. Even a negative, painful role will give this sense of belonging, a place to "fit." It feels better to belong as a scapegoat than to feel totally alone.

Young Scapegoats

The scapegoat role may develop in a number of ways. The Jones family is a fairly typical example. Robert and Mary had been married three years. While their marriage had been rather stormy, they were both devoted parents to their fourteen-month-old son, Bobby. Robert and Mary came in for marriage counseling to improve their skills in conflict resolution. Progress was slow and laborious; emotional defenses were high for both of them.

In the course of therapy they discovered an interesting pattern that had been developing for some time. Generally a cooperative and compliant child, Bobby would sometimes act in direct disobedience to his parents. Since consistent discipline was a high priority for both Robert and Mary, Bobby's disobedience was dealt with immediately. His parents were careful to be both firm and loving in their response. Despite their earnest attempts at responding appropriately, Bobby's "rebellious streak" persisted. His parents' patience and energy were wearing thin.

One day Robert and Mary noticed something almost by accident. While discussing Bobby's discipline, they both realized that his misbehavior occurred inevitably when there was tension between the two of them. They observed that as they began to disagree and their tone of voice rose, Bobby would do something "naughty." He might run over and play with the stereo, climb onto the kitchen counter, or break something. His specific behavior would vary, but it was always something for which he knew he would be punished. At that point his parents would stop arguing, turn their attention toward Bobby, and deal with his misbehavior. At this point the tension was broken, and they seldom returned to their original conflict. At fourteen months of age Bobby was learning an important lesson that all scapegoats learn: "If this family is to survive, I must get into trouble." It worked like a charm. Although no one was noticing it, a young family scapegoat was beginning to emerge. Unless something changed, Bobby would probably soon be known as the kid with the behavior problem.

Recognizing this process became the motivation Robert and Mary needed to work toward resolving their differences. They stopped allowing Bobby to divert their attention from conflict. They made sure that reaching a solution became the norm in their house. They also committed themselves to expressing affection and affirmation to each other, in Bobby's presence, at the conclusion of their conflicts.

Not surprisingly, Bobby's strategic misbehaviors ended. Almost secondarily, Robert and Mary found that their marriage improved tremendously. While the example of Bobby is fairly typical, it is by no means the only way a scapegoat develops. If one of the parents grew up as the family scapegoat, chances are good that he or she will continue that role as an adult. If neither parent was a scapegoat but both grew up in families where scapegoats existed, they will probably "scapegoat" one of the children—often the firstborn. In both of these scenarios, a family pattern of dealing with tension by scapegoating is carried into the new family.

If one child threatens the self-esteem of the family, perhaps due to a handicap of some sort, there is a good possibility that he or she may become designated as the "problem." If the child is retarded or overly intelligent, unattractive or especially attractive, or in any way "different" from the other family members, that unique quality may become a factor in that person's becoming a family scapegoat. The "differentness" may be a family member's temperament. If one member is too aggressive or too passive, too dependent or too autonomous, these factors may predispose one individual to be scapegoated. Sometimes even being named after or resembling some past scapegoat may designate the role. Though the roots of the role may vary a great deal, the results are remarkably similar.

Adult Scapegoats

Like family heroes, scapegoats generally carry the characteristics they develop in childhood into adulthood and they continue to play their familiar role in other relationships. The role of scapegoat served a purpose in the family of origin, even though it was negative—it served to reduce tension and give the child an identity within the family. Yet once that role is carried outside the family, it often wreaks havoc in new relationships, as well as life in general.

Adult scapegoats often find it difficult to feel at ease in any situation. When they are successful at something, they tend to feel the vague discomfort of an unfamiliar setting, as if they don't belong. When they fail or are rejected in some way, they feel a frustration and anger that is familiar—but certainly not satisfying.

Though the scapegoat may appear apathetic or even self-righteous, especially as a teenager, this behavior is a facade. The family scapegoat feels deeply guilty, lonely, and helpless. In spite of a desire to do well, he or she feels almost compelled toward self-defeating, self-destructive behavior, as if being swept along by a current he or she doesn't understand, propelled by the responses of others who are often oblivious to the process.

The Family Mascot

Greg first came to my office at the request of his employer. According to his boss, this twenty-eight-year-old sales representative did an excellent job but was extremely difficult to work with. While his customers loved him, his co-workers could hardly tolerate him. In our first session Greg appeared to be a warm, open, likable fellow. Judging from this first impression, it was hard to imagine why this young man had been through seven jobs in five years and was already into his third marriage. In every situation, whether job change or marriage breakup, Greg felt someone else was to blame. He had many good, logical reasons as to why his chronic relationship problems were caused by the failure of others.

Greg was the youngest of three children. His parents, John and Doris, had tried for many years to have children but had been unable to conceive. Eventually they adopted two girls and began adapting to the routines of family life.

When the younger daughter was ten years old, Greg's mother learned she was pregnant. Doris was the youngest child in a very close family of eight children and everyone was excited about this miracle child. Since Doris was forty years old, concerns ran high and everyone watched the pregnancy closely.

Greg was born strong and healthy, with a ready-made fan club. Not only was he the long-awaited birth child of John and Doris and the cuddly baby brother of his much-older sisters, but he was also the youngest of seventeen grandchildren by ten years! Needless to say, he was doted on, cooed over, constantly played with, overprotected, underdisciplined, and generally coddled and spoiled by innumerable people throughout childhood. Everyone enjoyed Greg, and Greg enjoyed being enjoyed.

The result of this wonderful childhood was that Greg entered adulthood with virtually no experience in difficult relationships. Greg had never learned to adapt or adjust to anyone. "This is how I am; take it or leave it!" was one of his favorite lines. His outlook on life was self-centered, and his relationships were hollow. Yet through his childhood experiences Greg *had* developed some very valuable skills in building relationships. He had learned to be charming, pleasantly superficial, and powerfully manipulative. He built relationships quickly, and people naturally liked him. But these relationships could not move beyond a superficial level, and eventually Greg's high expectations for others and egocentric perspective took its toll. Friends burned out and moved on, as did jobs and wives. Because of Greg's ability to project blame onto others, he was usually able to convince a significant number of people that his previous problems belonged to someone else. His biggest problem was that he was able to convince himself of the same thing.

Greg stayed in therapy for several sessions, all of which were paid for by his employer. In one particular session Greg was confronted about inappropriate behavior toward a boss. Following this session he decided there were better job opportunities available; he quit his job without notice and didn't return to therapy.

The Mascot Role

A family mascot tends to be the focus of everyone else's attention. The nurturing the mascot receives is not necessarily earned or deserved. The family mascot achieves the role not because of anything he or she has done but because of other factors, which may include:

Being the youngest of the siblings, especially if much younger.
Being the smallest or "cutest."
Being more frail, disabled, or needy in some way.
Being the only boy in a family of girls, or vise versa.

Regardless of which attribute elicits attention, one characteristic is universal for all mascots: Less maturity and independence is expected of the mascot than of other siblings. The mascot can often "get away with murder"—that is, actions other siblings would be reprimanded for are excused or minimized. These factors have a powerful effect on the development of the mascot's personality.

Adult Mascots

Mascots learn early in life that they are likable. That basic assumption affects their response to others in many ways. They are generally talkative and sociable, often becoming "the life of the party" in groups. They learn to use their charismatic charm advantageously. Often family mascots are notorious manipulators, knowing how to get what they want. While they may be effective in passively controlling situations, they generally do not assume leadership well and are usually uncomfortable if designated "the boss."

As adults, mascots tend to be outgoing, spontaneous people-pleasers. They usually reflect self-confidence and handle social situations well. Family mascots are usually fun to be around. The skills learned in their families of origin are well suited to the fields of marketing, sales, and public relations, which is where many mascots end up. On the negative side, mascots have a tendency to be emotionally dependent and self-centered with a strong need for the approval of others. Though very conscious of what others think of them, their spontaneous reactions may give the impression that they don't care. They tend to relinquish responsibility easily. They seem to assume that whatever they leave undone will somehow get done or won't matter. Often impulsive, their lifestyles can be chaotic and unstable—that is, unless they marry lieutenants or rescuers (which they often do), in which case they generally trade instability for power struggles in marriage. Mascots often seem to search for partners to nurture, guide, and control them, since such relationships allow them to play their mascot role.

Additional Roles

The roles mentioned in this chapter are certainly not the only ones that exist. In fact, the list of possible family roles is probably endless. As you explore your own family, feel free to define and name whatever role you feel best describes a particular individual. Following are some other examples of very common family roles.

The Lost Child

Typically a middle child (not first or last born), "the lost child" deals with tension by withdrawing from or avoiding the family. This family member usually has his or her closest relationships outside the family. The most likely to be overlooked or neglected by the family, this person finds it hard to relax in relationships because fundamental trust has never been established within the family. In adulthood this person has difficulty drawing close to others and has few, if any, intimate relationships. The fear of rejection tends to control a great deal of this person's behavior.

The Mediator

The "mediator" is the family member who always seems to be in the middle of family confrontations, trying to bring the opposing sides together. Since family members tend to rely on this person to help them resolve their own problems, his or her identity becomes very wrapped up in the needs of others. He or she often has no concrete sense of personal needs, preferences, or priorities. In adulthood this person typically is well liked and has many friends. But since most of these relationships are based on problems, he or she has few true peers and enjoys very little mutual sharing of needs. Actually, this popular person often feels very lonely.

The Family Clown

The "family clown" deals with tension through humor. When there is anger or conflict within the family, the family clown will crack a joke, make a snide comment, or act out some humorous antic. Sometimes the clown will relieve family tension at his or her own expense. When the laughter is a response to self-criticism or self-deprecation, the family is sacrificing this member to avoid its own tension. Such humor may be very uncomfortable for an outsider to watch, but the family may be unaware of what's happening.

As an adult, the family clown is very difficult to get close to emotionally because he or she has learned that emotional intensity should be avoided. Though this person may draw many acquaintances to his or her lighthearted approach to life, intimate friendships are rare. The family clown may be fun to be around, but you often sense that you never really know this person.

Role Changes

Family roles are not unchangeable. In fact, changes in formal family roles are traditionally announced and celebrated. A wedding is such a celebration. The bride and groom are taking on new formal roles and (to some degree, anyway) letting go of old roles. Graduations, baby showers, and even funerals are ways of announcing formal role changes. Of course, these role changes affect all family members in many ways and may even cause changes in some of the family's informal roles. Each of these occasions changes the expectations of the people involved.

Informal family roles may also change as a family grows. Remember the model of family as a mobile that adjusts to find a new equilibrium when "knocked" by change. A teenage girl who has always called her mother "Mommy" and begins to address her as "Mother" is indicating a desire for a change in role. She wants to be viewed and treated differently. A six-year-old child who gets a newborn sibling and suddenly regresses to crawling, talking like a toddler, or wanting to be rocked to sleep is expressing a discomfort with the role change to older sibling. If the six-year-old has been the family mascot, the newborn may become the object of jealousy and anger.

Examining the Clues

Exploring informal family roles may involve more than just examining the behavior of family members. Clues can be found in other characteristics displayed by family members.

Family nicknames can point to family roles. An adult who still responds to a childish name may be continuing to play an old role. This is especially true if the name is used only by the family of origin. For example, a successful corporate vice-president whose parents and siblings continue to call him "Spanky" may have a family who wants him to maintain a familiar role even though it is inconsistent with the rest of his life. How he responds to that name may indicate the strength of his own desire for that familiar role. If he responds positively, he may be indicating his preference for the old "Spanky" role. If, on the other hand, he becomes irritable or confrontational around his family, he may be showing his desire to change from the old role, even if he's not consciously aware of it. A derogatory or demeaning nickname may indicate a family scapegoat. The member with such a name will often live as though he or she expects to live out the description.

Sometimes a child will resemble an older family member who had a particular role. Such a resemblance may be a factor in assuming or assigning that informal role. A child who is regularly told that he looks exactly like Uncle Herman will spend time thinking about

Uncle Herman. If Uncle Herman was an alcoholic who spent twenty-five years in prison, that life scenario will affect the child's view of himself. If family members constantly remind the child of the resemblance, it may indicate their expectations for that child to take over the role. The same principle may apply to a child who has been given the name of an older family member.

A family member who has some sort of special characteristic, such as a disability or a special gift, or is known as the tallest, shortest, heaviest, strongest, angriest, or kindest person in the family may have a unique informal family role. When you identify someone in your family with a particular role, pay attention to how various family members relate to this person—other roles may begin to emerge.

Snow White

The story of Snow White gives a good summary of how family roles function. We're all familiar with the story of the helpless princess, the wicked queen, and the handsome prince. This story is a good example for several reasons. First, because the roles in the story are "larger than life"—crystal clear and distinct. Second, it illustrates the fact that if any role were removed, the flow of the entire story would necessarily be altered. What the story does not show us is that the roles played cause us to make assumptions, ignore facts, and draw conclusions that may be distortions of reality. Let's take a look at some of the characters and their roles.

The Wicked Queen/Witch

The Wicked Witch plays a central part in the story. Actually, there could be no story without her. Her purpose is to be the focus of trouble. Her role is made distinct because there is not one shred of goodness portrayed in her. She is so bad that everyone else looks good by comparison. Our expectations are for her to be negative and despicable, and she seems to fulfill them all. That's a pretty tough role to be put into. She must have had a painful childhood.

The Woodman

The Woodman plays the role of guardian or protector in the story. He is portrayed as being heroic, loving, and just. Our emotional response to him is gratitude and respect. Who would think of questioning his integrity? Apparently no one wonders why this strong, wonderful man chooses the employment of this horrid queen. He's obviously a real manipulator. Why do we feel such approval when he betrays her, lies to her, and continues to work for her? It's probably because we've already identified her as the villain, and there's only room for one. Besides, he's nice to Snow White, and we all like her. Frankly, I think he gets away with a lot. I wouldn't trust him.

Snow White

The princess is an interesting character. We all love her for some inexplicable reason. In terms of the story, she is a character almost devoid of substance. Her only purpose in the story is to be the focus of everyone else's attention. She doesn't do a thing, really. We all attribute wonderful characteristics to her even though she doesn't demonstrate any. We assume traits such as innocence, purity, and honesty when what we actually see is passivity. In fact, we ignore a lot of pretty negative things. She doesn't seem to give a second thought to moving in to live with seven single men whom she's just met, yet no one questions her morality. That type of attitude certainly doesn't develop overnight! How did she get the name Snow White when her hair is so black?

The Seven Dwarfs

These guys play the role of nurturant providers. They also provide a bit of comic relief in an otherwise dull story. They are portrayed as benevolent, innocent, and hardworking. Here again, most people seem to take that image at face value and ignore the obvious. Why do they live in this messy little shack when they're in the diamond business? What do they do with all their money? Here are seven men dealing in precious gems—with incredibly low overhead. Yet they live in squalor and isolation. Looks pretty suspicious to me.

The Prince

The prince in the story has an amazing effect on us. Most young girls grow up dreaming about being swept away by someone just like him. We view him as strong, dynamic, and heroic. The entire story builds toward his entrance onto the set. We all admire him. All of this in spite of the fact that he says absolutely nothing. He shows up in the final scene after all threats of danger have passed. He makes sexual advances toward a sleeping woman he's never seen before, and then he vanishes with woman in tow. I find it hard to believe that this is the first time he's been so forward. I wonder how many other women have been to his palace? I wonder how many are still there? I'd certainly never let my daughter date a guy like that!

Isn't it interesting that as mature, reasoning adults, almost no one has considered the obvious distortions in the characters of this familiar story? Though the discrepancies are clear for any adult to see, it never occurs to most of us to challenge or even question the basic assumptions of this familiar story. The same process of passively accepting that which is familiar has a powerful effect on many areas of our lives.

From Milk to Meat

If you have recognized familiar family patterns while reading this chapter, perhaps it is time for you to identify and choose to live beyond the role you lived out as a child and to uncover the false assumptions that you hold toward others in your family. In 1 Corinthians 13:11, the apostle Paul makes an interesting comment about maturity: "When I was a child, I used to speak as a child, think as a child, reason as a child; when I became a man, I did away with childish things." He is saying that growing to maturity involves letting go of childhood perspectives. He was well aware that our reasoning process does not necessarily mature naturally as we age physically. In 1 Corinthians 3:2 Paul points out that the Corinthians were still functioning spiritually as children, even though they had all the resources they needed to become mature: "I gave you milk to drink, not solid food; for you were not yet able to receive it." Hebrews 5:12–14 makes a similar point—that maturity includes acting on mature perspectives.

What these biblical writers teach us about spiritual growth also applies to our emotional development. Leaving childhood behind involves learning to view ourselves and our world more fully and realistically. This is an active process; it seldom happens passively. It occurs because we make a conscious decision to change and begin actively working toward that change. Without decisive action, it is natural to continue in our familiar, childhood patterns of perception and reaction.

Childish Thinking

It shouldn't surprise us that we readily accept what we are told as children. What is amazing is that we are so slow to question these messages as we grow older. Many of the things we learn as children are obviously untrue. Many of them probably affect how we live, how we perceive ourselves, and how we respond to others. Unfortunately, many of those false assumptions have never changed.

Thus it is with many family roles. We learned them in childhood, when they served a purpose. Too often we carry them with us into adulthood and continue to play them long after their usefulness has ended. They often cause trouble for us without our even realizing that they exist.

As you sort through your own family history, look carefully at the characteristics and behaviors of each family member. Watch how each interplays with the others. Don't restrict yourself to the roles specifically discussed here, but feel free to identify any role that seems appropriate to you. Give each role whatever name you believe best describes it. Take time to ponder and examine each role and how it fits into the rest of the family. Look through old family photos and see which family roles are most evident in them.

If you have a family member or close family friend with whom you feel comfortable discussing the following questions, such a conversation may help you identify and explore various roles.

Your Personal Family Voyage

Looking Back

Think about the personality characteristics and typical behaviors of each member of your family of origin. If possible, give each role, including your own, a specific name. Then answer the following questions.

1. How did each role affect you as a child in that family?

2. How did each parent interact with each role?

3. How did those interactions affect your own role in the family?

4. What emotional reaction do you now have to your position and role in your family of origin?

Looking Forward

5. In what specific ways do you still play out your family role?

6. What responses do you notice in others that are reactions to your own family role as identified above?

7. What is the greatest benefit you currently derive from this role?

8. What is the biggest problem this role causes you in relationships today?

9. If you were to decide to change this role in some way, what behaviors would you expect to need to change? How would these changes affect others around you?

5

Family Rules

In the same way that family *roles*
give each family member a place
to "fit" into the family identity,
family *rules* tell each member
how to play his or her part.
Some rules are very clear
and understandable;
some are extremely
clouded and confusing.

He must think I'm stupid!" Joan's eyes filled with tears as her tone intensified. "He tells me how to clean, how to shop, how to decorate. I can't plan a meal without his changing it. He has something to say about everything I do. I feel as if I can't do anything that's good enough for him." She paused to regain composure. "He's a hard worker, and I'm thankful for his income. It allows me to stay home, raise our children, and manage our household. But that's almost impossible to do when he has to control everything."

"It's Joan who has to control everything." There was a weariness in Bill's voice. "I can't make a suggestion or correct anything without her reacting as if she's being abused. If I give her any input at all, she thinks I'm trying to push her around. She has absolutely no respect for me or my opinions. Sometimes I think she wants me to just give her my paycheck and stay out of her life."

The conflict between Bill and Joan is certainly not uncommon or bizarre. It is, however, very frustrating for each of the spouses who feels so helpless to change their relationship. Each person perceives the partner's response as unreasonable and overreactive, and to some degree both are correct. However, without an understanding of the *source* of these reactions, it will be very difficult for these two to find a more satisfying balance in their relationship.

Bill and Joan had two very different sets of assumptions, though neither was consciously aware of them. Both sets seemed to work well in their respective families of origin, but they brought constant tension when combined in this new family. Since these sets of expectations had become so natural for each of them, it never occurred to Bill or Joan to explore them together.

Bill's mother grew up with very little freedom. As the youngest child with three brothers, she was carefully protected and supervised throughout childhood. She married an older man whom she and her family respected and who was very comfortable continuing the patterns of her parents and siblings. The result of this union was a family that placed Father at the "hub" of family life. Bill, then, grew up with a set of unspoken assumptions regarding Dad:

1. Dad was wise, mature, and insightful, and therefore was consulted about everything.
2. Dad, as head of the home, was never to be directly confronted about anything.
3. Dad's word was final in all facets of home life.

These unspoken expectations were very clear in Bill's family. As an adult Bill unconsciously measured his success as husband and father by how well these expectations were applied to him. Of course, Bill did not consciously believe that these were appropriate measures of successful leadership in the home. Because the learning process had been so subtle, it had never before occurred to him that he was living according to these rules.

Both of Joan's parents were successful professionals. Independence, hard work, and achievement were highly valued in her family. The family held high expectations for these characteristics among its members. As a result both she and her younger brother were given responsibility early in life.

Since business took Dad away from home a good deal, Joan's mother was responsible for raising the children and managing the household along with her career. She was successful in everything she did, including passing on to her firstborn daughter her strong sense of independence and competence. By the time Joan was eight years old, she could cook dinner for the family and clean the entire house if she had to. By age ten she would plan the family's weekly menu and do the shopping. She was an excellent student and an accomplished pianist. Joan grew up with two very clear, though unspoken assumptions:

1. To be successful, you must be able to function without anyone's help.
2. To be loved and accepted, you must perform your duties successfully.

In therapy Bill was able to verbalize the fact that he felt minimized by Joan's independence. He came to realize that he took it as a statement of his failure and inadequacy as head of their home. Joan felt minimized by his leadership style, interpreting it as criticism and rejection of her as a person and a wife. As a result, while Bill was unconsciously waiting to be consulted about household details (in order to show love to his wife), Joan was working hard to please him with her capability and success. Each experienced the other's attempts to please as rejection.

When they finally examined this aspect of their families of origin, many of their struggles seemed to resolve themselves. The reason behind this practically effortless resolution of conflict? It became clear that they were not adversaries in these issues: Their differing reactions now had a context that went beyond their marriage. Each could understand the other's behavior as loving and caring. As they learned to understand and empathize with each other's history, defenses came down and behaviors became less annoying and more open to change.

Rules and More Rules

"Why do I do that? It doesn't make sense!" Have you ever asked that of yourself? Most of us have. Behind this question lies the understanding that all behavior has a cause. No human response is absurd regardless of how ridiculous it appears. Each person's behavior, decisions, and reactions emerge from a context of some sort. This frame of reference, if it is understood, can shine a spotlight into a dark area that is otherwise baffling. In this chapter we will explore family rules which are the motivation for many things we seem to do automatically.

In essence, family rules are the way family values are passed on from one generation to another. Through rules, a family communicates its expectations for family members as well as for those out-side the family. Rules tell us what is acceptable and unacceptable, proper and improper, good and bad. Family rules communicate expectations about how people are to relate to one another, how the different generations are to interact, and what is expected of each individual. In the same way that family *roles* give each member a place to "fit" into the family identity, family *rules* tell each member how to play his or her part. Some rules are very clear and understandable; some are extremely clouded and confusing. Since families have expectations about everything they do, they also have rules about everything they do. Very often family members aren't aware of many of these rules until they come into conflict with someone whose rules are different from their own.

Every family has what I call "written rules"—expectations that have been communicated directly in some way. They are clearly understood by each family member and can be openly discussed by all. Written rules give structure and stability to family life. They include things such as table manners, curfews, and chores.

"Finish your dinner or no dessert."
"Do your homework before you go out to play."
"Bedtime is ten o'clock."

Because they can be discussed, written rules can be confronted and evaluated. As a result of this direct interaction, from time to time they change.

Unwritten rules are quite another story. These rules consistently influence behavior within the family but have never been directly stated. Although these repeated patterns of interaction within a family may not be carried out on a conscious level, they are observable and predictable. In fact, they are usually most apparent to an observant outsider. Because they occur consistently, family members expect these patterns to continue. These unspoken expectations are not open for discussion or evaluation, generally because no one is consciously aware of them. While they may not be talked about, and at times their existence may even be denied, the family's behavior shows that they are understood very well by the family members.

Families have unwritten rules about all kinds of things. The most readily visible rules are those regarding emotional tension. If the children misbehave or cause distraction whenever the parents argue, they are communicating the rule "Parents can't fight." If parents take over a task or job for a child whenever he or she complains or experiences difficulty, then the rule may be "Children can't be frustrated." If family members act differently around a particular parent, treating them "with kid gloves," the rule may be "Mom (or Dad) must not get angry." Because unwritten rules are not verbalized, family members may often be unaware they exist. Since they are not open for discussion or debate, they seldom change without some sort of significant turmoil.

Family rules accomplish several purposes. For one, they serve to regulate tension within the family. Too much tension or conflict within a home makes family life chaotic, unsettled, and insecure, but, since emotional tension is a necessary part of growth and change, too little tension results in stagnation and indifference. The level of tension one may call "healthy" will vary from family to family depending on expectations and responses of family members.

Another purpose served by family rules is that of defining the family's identity. Rules help members to experience themselves as a unit. They give the family a sense of uniqueness. As mentioned earlier, family identity is a primary factor in the unity and cohesiveness between family members.

A third purpose for family rules is possibly the most obvious: Rules lend stability and predictability to family life. Rules tell me where I stand, even if I disagree with them—even if I violate them. Surprisingly, this is true even if the specific rules have never been verbalized.

Good News and Bad News

The good news about family rules is that they help make family life stable and predictable. They help keep the family "mobile" balancing. Rules are a big part of the emotional equilibrium that every family seeks. The bad news is that family rules can keep family members from growing, maturing, and changing. This is especially true for rules that limit communication or emotional closeness. It is also true for rules that are arbitrary and overly rigid.

Some rules help us prepare for and live in the adult world, the world "out there" beyond our family. These tend to be functional, helpful rules that lead us toward emotional independence and maturity. These also tend to be rules that apply to life in general. They teach us to understand others, express ourselves appropriately, resolve problems, communicate clearly, and care about relationships.

Other unwritten rules apply only to life within the family. They teach us very little about life in general; in fact, they often distort our perspective of life. These rules are often bound up in our parents' own histories and families of origin. As adults we continue to be loyal to these rules until we consciously change them.

A number of speakers have shared a story that is an excellent example of this process. Preparing a company meal, a young bride sliced off an end piece of the raw roast and discarded it. Curious as to why she would throw away what appeared to be a perfectly good piece of meat, her husband asked her why she would do such a thing. She had a perfectly good reason: "Because that's the way Mom always did it."

Sometime later, while they were visiting the wife's family, the husband asked his mother-in-law why she had discarded the slice of meat. Her answer sounded familiar: "Oh, my mother always prepared it that way."

By now this young man was pretty curious. His wife's grandmother was still living, so he gave her a call, explaining that since this technique of throwing away a slice of the roast was traced back to her, he was interested in her insights.

She gave a quick, clear answer: "My roasting pan was too small for a whole roast." Two generations of wasted meat—all because of an unspoken assumption. It points out a profound truth about families: Things that seem natural to us may not be natural at all; often it takes a "view from the outside" to see what actually occurs within our own family.

Unwritten Rules

The most influential rules in our families are the unwritten ones—those based on assumptions. Their communication has been subtle and has occurred over a long period time. It is clear that these rules have been communicated because family members live by them consistently.

Let's imagine a hypothetical family—the Joneses—eating dinner. Ten-year-old Johnny becomes angry over something someone says. He gets up, runs to his room, and closes the door. With this behavior, Johnny has both broken and enforced an unwritten family rule: Anger is unacceptable; we are not an angry family. Since the breaking of unwritten rules is generally punished by rejection, this boy enforces the rule by leaving the family. (If he hadn't left the table, another family member may have asked him to leave.)

We can confidently assume this pattern didn't begin with this incident. It has probably existed for years, possibly for generations. Some of the effects of this rule on family members will be fairly predictable. We could expect them to be intolerant of anger in anyone, even nonfamily members. They probably feel guilty when they become angry and are critical when they see others express anger. Each family member will learn unique ways to express these uncomfortable emotions; the form of that expression will depend on the person's role in the family and the particular situation. Yet within the family the internal (emotional) reaction to anger will be fairly consistent.

It is usually easier to identify unwritten family rules in someone else's family than in your own. In fact, the most difficult family to examine objectively will probably be your own family of origin. This may be partially because we are protective and loyal to our families. But primarily it's because we've lived with the rules so long, it doesn't occur to us that they exist.

Unwritten rules are generally enforced through rejection by parents and family members. Controlling children through rejection can be done with direct statements:

"Mommy doesn't love you when you act like that."

"You are an awful child when you do that."
"If you act (talk, feel) like that, you're no child of mine."

Rejection and control can also be expressed indirectly:

"I won't talk to you when you're crying (angry, depressed)."
"Go to your room if you feel that way."
"I won't be around you when you're like that."

The common factor in both expressions of rejection is the under-lying message: "You will be loved and considered worthy only if you perform properly." Behavior is not separated from the individual: Bad behavior equals a bad person. The result is a sense of shame and fear of abandonment.

Adults raised with this form of discipline can find it hard to imagine any other method of response to a child's inappropriate behavior. An alternative message would be: "I love you regardless of what you do, but there are negative consequences for your inappropriate behavior." In this case parental love and acceptance are not withheld, and consequences for behavior are separated from the child as a person.

To a young child, the threat of rejection or abandonment is a powerful motivator. Physically dependent on parents and authority figures, children have a strong need to please them. Something as subtle as a facial gesture, the refusal of a hug, or silence can elicit fear and shame in a young child. When the threat of rejection is used regularly and consistently in a child's life, that child becomes sensitized to rejection. He or she develops a habit of avoiding rejection at all costs, which will carry over into adulthood long after the child becomes independent and no longer needs parents for physical survival.

Adults who were raised with many rigidly enforced unwritten rules often will go to great lengths to avoid the anxiety associated with disapproval—even to the point of injuring themselves physically, emotionally, or spiritually. We will examine this pattern in more detail in chapter 8.

Even in homes where the use of rejection is neither chronic nor severe, rejection, though unintentional, is the primary enforcer of unwritten rules. As you explore this area of your family history, watch for the subtle forms of rejection that may have molded your perceptions and reactions.

The variety of unwritten rules within families is limitless, but an examination of a few common issues will serve as a sampling of how unwritten rules work. Let's explore some of the general areas into which unwritten rules typically fall.

Expressing Emotions

For Ken to see his wife cry was an unnerving experience. Whenever she cried he felt a strong need to stop her and smooth things out somehow. For Catherine, crying was a soothing release of tension. She felt minimized and patronized when Ken would try to squelch her tears, and she interpreted his lack of observable emotion as apathy. It was hard for her to feel she was important to him when he expressed no emotion. It wasn't until each began to understand the other's family rules that their reactions began to change. Eventually they each learned to take these reactions less personally. This freed each of them to express emotion naturally without the defensiveness of the other.

Most families have unwritten rules about the expression of various emotions. The communication of feelings can cause great upheaval and turmoil in families unless there is balance. When there are no limits on how emotions are expressed, people can be hurt, violated, and abused. When expression of feelings is forbidden, those feelings tend to come out in other, generally unhealthy, ways. The honest expression of feelings needs to be balanced with courtesy and respect for others. While it is unrealistic to deny the existence of anger, it is likewise inappropriate to physically or verbally abuse another person. While most families have limits in this area, others tend to be rigid.

Typically, the unwritten rules regarding expression revolve around "forbidden" emotions:

"It is wrong to make another person uncomfortable. We do not
confront one another."

"We are a positive, joyful family. No one may express negative
emotions such as anger, sadness, fear, or hurt."

"The women in our family are gentle. They may not be angry,
but they may be depressed."

"The men in our family are strong. They may not be fearful or
hurt, but they may be angry."

"We are a loving family. We do not have conflict or disagree
with one another."

This type of family rule tends to affect family members in two
ways. First, emotional experiences become confused. When genuine feelings are minimized, denied, or redefined, a child's emotional experience becomes distorted. Believing that anger or sadness
is bad does not make it less real. The child learns to distrust the
senses and becomes confused—anger isn't really anger; hurt isn't
really hurt. When children experience a forbidden emotion, they
feel guilty and ashamed as though they themselves are somehow
"bad." They then deny the emotion to avoid the shame. When emotions are denied consistently, as a way of life, they tend to come
out "sideways," in some form that does not violate the family rule.
Rules suppressing emotions often produce adults who may be convinced that they harbor no anger, but their depression, ulcers, or
migraine headaches tell another story.

Second, family members learn to develop emotional distance.
When someone cannot or will not express strong feelings, other
people have a hard time getting to know that person very well.
Genuine intimacy becomes impossible and most relationships are
artificial and shallow. Families with restrictive rules governing
honest emotional interaction are often communicating to one
another that emotional stability is valued more highly than emotional closeness. While the emotional temperature in the home
may be low, the emotional investment among members is generally low as well.

Success and Failure

Anyone who knew Mike would describe him as a difficult person. He was friendly enough at first, though very nervous. He was a good conversationalist and could listen well to the concerns of others. People tended to like Mike on their first meeting. In his job as a finish carpenter, he was recognized as the best. His work was immaculate and flawless. Though he worked slowly and was expensive to hire, his customers sang his praises.

Once a relationship moved beyond superficial conversation, however, it became obvious that Mike was chronically discontented. He had something subtly negative to say about everything and everyone. His outlook on life was pessimistic and burdened. His personal involvements with people were few. He seemed to avoid commitments and obligations of any kind. Just below the surface, Mike was a fearful and lonely man.

When Mike began therapy with the goal of developing some stress-management skills, he quickly discovered that the source of his stress was within himself. By every definition of the term he was a perfectionist. His high standards of performance led him to avoid any situation with potential for failure. These expectations also gave him a low tolerance for the shortcomings of others. The results? Avoidance and isolation.

On a journey through his past, Mike discovered within his family an endless set of rigid rules for the performance of children. Every facet of his childhood behavior was governed by regulations and penalties. It was surprising for him to realize that he was still living by those outdated standards from his past. Fearful of consequences that no longer existed, he was attempting to live up to standards he realized were unreasonable. This discovery was truly life-changing for Mike, who is now developing a new set of rules of his own choosing and according to his own values. It's a slow process and requires a good deal of self-awareness, but in spite of the time and effort involved, Mike will tell you he'd never go back.

Many families have strict unwritten rules regarding standards of performance by family members. Examples of these may be:

"Whatever you do, it must be done correctly."
"There's only one way to do things—the right way!"
"To fail in any way is a shameful thing."

These rules are learned clearly and quickly through regular, consistent criticism and minimal affirmation. Criticism may be communicated directly, through complaints and condemnation of what a child does or how the child acts, or indirectly, through disapproving frowns, silence, or regularly comparing the child to someone or something "better."

The definition of what is "correct" or "perfect" may vary widely. One family may define "correct" as being sociable. Having many friends and no enemies would be correct in this family. Conflict then would be a measure of failure. Another family may define "correct" as remaining separate from "the world." In this family a very small circle of social contacts would be considered appropriate and positive. A family member with a broad spectrum of friends might be an embarrassment to the family that considers such liberal relationships an indication of moral decay or spiritual failure.

One family might measure "correctness" in financial terms. A nice home, new cars, and many possessions would spell success. The absence of these things may be cause for criticism or pity. Another family may define "correct" behavior as the absence of materialism. A simple lifestyle free of nonessential luxuries is the only one approved within this family that views expensive possessions with condemnation and disdain.

The values behind these rules may be positive and appropriate, but all too often these underlying motivations get lost when conformity becomes more highly valued than individuality. The performance of family members becomes more important than the people themselves.

Whatever the specifics within the family, the definition of "right," "correct," or "perfect" is always dependent on a comparison. To be defined, "perfect" must be contrasted with "imperfect." Because there must always be a "wrong" to avoid at all costs, there is a judg-mental attitude or a "better than others" aspect to this rule, even though it may be vehemently denied.

This necessary comparison sets up a system of competition for the family. This competition affects not only how the family views outsiders, but how family members view one another. Since being "wrong" results in shame and being "right" is merely expected, avoid-ing being wrong often becomes more important than doing what is right. Defensiveness, blame, justification, and rationalization are typ-ical patterns in families with perfectionistic performance rules.

The long-term effect of these rules is twofold. First a child devel-ops a mental image as to what he or she "should be" and strives constantly to achieve it. Usually this ideal standard cannot be achieved, at least consistently. As a result of this, the child becomes self-critical, discontent, and defensive—a perfectionist. Second, the child learns to project expectations and perfectionism onto others. Since others cannot fulfill the expectations, the child is disappointed and critical. This child is demanding, condemning, nagging, and rejecting. He or she feels hurt and in turn hurts others, alienating them and damaging close relationships.

Physical Expression of Affection

Eric can't remember ever seeing his parents touch each other. He certainly felt loved and cared for as a child, but that love wasn't expressed through hugs. In his family, affection was expressed through giving gifts and other tangible ways, such as doing special favors. His wife, Rosa, grew up with constant physical affection from her family. Touching among family members was a natural part of any conversation. The difference had become a joke between them. Eric humorously observed that anytime they were with her family, someone had a hand on him. He felt like a new teddy bear in a roomful of toddlers.

Early in their marriage Eric and Rosa were each offended by the other's approach to this dissimilarity. She felt neglected and he felt smothered. Five years and many heated discussions later, each had adapted to the other's style of expression. As Eric and Rosa learned to understand each other's histories, their relationship had developed into a "hybrid" of these two families. They both were comfortable with the new balance.

The communication of affection is laden with family expectations. In some families, physical touch is uncomfortable and somewhat threatening. In other families, members feel rejected when a greeting isn't accompanied with an embrace. These expectations, often cultural and carried down through many generations, are rarely discussed openly.

Rules regarding physical expression of affection vary widely.

"Women may hug one another, men may only shake hands."
"Adults may hug children but never other adults."
"Physical affection is private, never to be shown in public."
"If you care for someone, you touch that person regularly."

Probably the most significant effect of these rules is on the marriages of the grown children, as family-of-origin rules regarding affection frequently differ between husband and wife. Because your experience of affection is often tied to your feelings of acceptance, and because you are generally unaware of your expectations, this can become an emotionally loaded issue in marriage.

Learning to Disobey

The example of Jesus' life sheds some light on family rules and one's responsibility for sorting out which need to be kept and which can be discarded. In Matthew 12:46–50, Jesus is teaching a crowd when he is called aside by his mother and siblings. In this situation, Jesus refuses to comply with his mother's request. As an adult Jesus chose to place his ministry above his childhood role and the family rules. Jesus demonstrated the result of emotionally leaving his family patterns and replacing them with mature priorities and decisions.

The process of leaving rules learned in childhood behind is difficult and calls for discernment. Not all rules are fit to be obeyed, but not all rules are dangerous and damaging, either. As you explore the rules from your past, you'll have to sort out which rules are helpful and which cause you problems. Family rules that are dysfunctional and unhealthy can usually be identified by two factors: They have little or no relationship to life outside the family, and family members are not able to discuss or evaluate them. Dysfunctional rules of this type are explored further in chapter 8.

Some of the unwritten rules from your family of origin are undoubtedly positive and helpful to you today. As you discover and identify these, consider how you can strengthen and develop them as you consciously apply them to new areas of your life.

Some of the rules you uncover may not be so welcome. You may find them lurking behind repetitive and annoying problems you've been unable to overcome or resolve. Here are some steps to begin dealing with these stubborn patterns. An example is given of a family rule that can be dealt with through these steps.

1. Give the rule a name. Identify it as specifically as possible.
   "I may never question the behavior or decision of an authority figure."
2. Describe the purpose served in your childhood by this rule.
   "It allowed my father to continue his impulsive and destructive spending without feeling the guilt of being a poor role model."
3. Find ways the rule may have been appropriate and helpful.
   "It gave me a sense of security in an insecure environment."
   "It reduced my involvement in my parents' fights."
4. Determine its negative impact on your perceptions today.
   "It keeps me from developing confidence in my own judgment."
   "It distorts my understanding of appropriate spending."
5. Identify its impact on your lifestyle today.
   "It causes me to passively accept unfair and inappropriate treatment by authority figures."
6. Identify situations when you are most affected by this rule.
   "When my boss, pastor, or father makes a statement or decision with which I disagree."
7. Choose a more appropriate rule.
   "I should respectfully express my differing opinion to leadership figures because my opinion is valid and worthwhile."
8. Decide on and practice an appropriate way to demonstrate this new rule.

"I appreciate your position, but I disagree. I think another viewpoint to consider is . . ."

As you begin to break away from inappropriate rules from your childhood, remember that the family is a system or a mobile. Change in one person causes changes in others. In one way or another people around you will be forced to adjust in response to your new reactions. This may be difficult for many people to accept, especially family members. Try not to be too threatened by defensiveness in others. If you are committed to positive personal change, those who love you will learn to accept and adapt to your growth. The appropriateness of your changes must be measured by your values, not by the reactions of others.

Your Personal Family Voyage

1. List two unwritten rules from your family of origin. In what ways were these rules communicated to you as a child? Are these rules you appreciate or resent? How do these rules affect you today?

2. List two unwritten rules you live by today. Are your feelings about each of these rules positive or negative? How do each of these rules affect people around you?

For Those Who Are Married

3. Name one unwritten rule from your spouse's family of origin. How does this rule affect your relationship today?

4. Name one unwritten rule from your *current* family. Would you be comfortable making this a *written*, discussed, open rule in your family? Why or why not? If not, it's likely that the rule is unhealthy. In what *specific* ways can you begin to change the rule?

6

The Value of When Birth Order

Your birth order impacts
virtually every area of your life.
As you explore your family positions,
you'll better understand the personalities
and choices that develop from them.

The timing of your entrance into your family has a profound impact on who you become. This is the underlying assumption of the study of sibling position or birth order. There's nothing magical or even particularly mysterious about our birth order, yet the study has fascinated researchers for years, and I expect it will fascinate and enlighten you as you journey through your past.

The impact of birth order has been evident since the beginning of time. As the original firstborn, Cain was fairly typical: He was critical and discontented, with a strong need to be in control. Like most firstborns, he got fed up with his younger sibling's getting all the approval, even to the extreme of becoming mankind's first murderer (Gen. 4:1–8).

Joseph was a favored lastborn, even though he was eventually usurped by a younger brother, Benjamin. Throughout childhood Joseph continued to enjoy the special attention typically given to a lastborn child, much to the frustration of all his middleborn brothers. Responsible and dominant, firstborn Reuben stepped in to save Joseph's life. Manipulative secondborn Judah was able to turn a profit of twenty shekels by negotiating between Reuben's conscience and his brothers' jealous hatred (Gen. 37).

Jacob, Esau, Moses, David, Andrew, Peter: Scripture is replete with individuals who carry the traits of their birth order. Each demonstrates the factors we see influencing families today.

The study of sibling position revolves around the fact that families change as they grow. The family responds to each child differently, depending on the family's stage of development. Since each child is treated uniquely in the context of the whole family system, the relationship between the child and the family as a whole develops uniquely. This particular relationship shapes a child's personality in many ways.

Your birth order impacts virtually every area of your life: career decisions, choice of spouse, how you respond to your children, what motivates or frustrates you, and how you spend your leisure time. As you explore your family positions, you'll better understand the personalities and choices that develop from them. In *The Birth Order Book,* Dr. Kevin Leman makes an excellent case for the study of birth order:

> As a practicing psychologist, I have used my training and research in birth order as a useful tool in helping people turn their lives around. Birth order information helps Mary understand why John is always so picky, and John gains insight into Mary's "little girl" ways, which are driving him more bonkers by the day. Birth order helps Mom and Dad get a handle on why ten-year-old Buford can go through life oblivious to his open fly and C+ average, while thirteen-year-old Hortense has straight As and a good start on an ulcer.
>
> I served for several years as Assistant Dean of Students at the University of Arizona and once asked a leading faculty member of the College of Architecture if he had ever paid any attention to where the college's faculty members came from as far as birth order was concerned. He gave me a blank stare and said, "I really do have to run, Kevin."
>
> It was probably a good six months before he stopped me on campus one day and said, "Say, do you remember that crazy question you asked me about where our architectural faculty came from? I finally decided to take an informal poll and found that almost every one of our faculty is either a firstborn male or the only child in the family."
>
> That was an eye-opener for my friend, but for me it only confirmed a basic birth order principle: People who like structure and order have a tendency to enter professions that are rather exacting. Architecture is one of those professions that pay off on being "perfect."
>
> It's also fascinating to compare birth orders in the media. Newspaper and magazine reporters—those who write for a living—tend to be firstborns. Announcers and anchorpersons on radio and television tend to be later born. You could probably make a very good guess that your zany weatherman on the six o'clock news is the baby in the family. He's a performer, a showman. He's the guy who can make a drizzle seem funny. Youngest children in the family are

often in the professions that require the ability to be "on stage" and to perform.[1]

Dorothy's Story

"We've worked hard to treat all of our children equally in our home! If our families have such an impact on us as adults, how could my boys turn out so differently?" questioned Dorothy, a woman who stopped to talk following a workshop I taught on family-of-origin issues.

I've heard these words from many parents who are baffled by the dramatic variances in their children's personalities. Dorothy was struggling through her own sorrow and confusion in the wake of her son's third divorce. Divorce was a foreign experience for her, something that had never occurred in her own family. She'd always held marriage as a sacred trust and taught her children to do the same. She was hurt by her son's almost flippant attitude toward his marital commitment.

Dorothy assured me that her question was not motivated by a desire to rescue or "fix" her son. As a sixty-two-year-old widow, she had learned to allow her three adult sons to take responsibility for their own decisions. The source of this conversation was her desire to understand the dynamics within her family.

Her eldest son, Ron, was a self-employed accountant who was married with two children, active in his church, financially successful, and well respected in his community. Dorothy felt close to Ron and enjoyed spending Sundays with his family.

Her middle son, Clark, was a contract negotiator in middle management of a large construction firm. He had more friends than anyone could count and seemed to be interested in almost everything. Though contact with his mother was minimal, he seemed happy in his marriage and content with life in general.

Dorothy's concerns surrounded Barry, the youngest son. At thirty-one, Barry seemed unable to settle into anything consistently. His third marriage had recently broken up and he was out

---

1. Kevin Leman, *The Birth Order Book*, (Grand Rapids: Fleming H. Revell, 1985), 12–13.

of work again. He was defensive when faced with the spiritual values of his parents and apathetic toward almost everything else.

Unfortunately Dorothy and I didn't have time to delve fully into the dynamics represented in her three sons. I was able to briefly describe the basic principles of sibling position and recommend a local family therapist for further consultation. Maybe Dorothy will read this chapter and discover that the differences in her sons are pretty typical.

The Complexity of Birth Order

As a family grows, the number of relationships and possible interactions within the system changes dramatically. For example, before the arrival of children the marriage relationship involves three interacting units—two individual "I's" and one couple "we" relationship, or interaction. When the first child is born, the number of units increases to seven—three individuals, three couples, and one triangle. With the addition of child number two, there are four individuals, six couples, four triangles, and a quadrangle, for a total of *fifteen* units. By the time there is a fourth child, the number of interactions exceeds fifty.

Each child is born into a family situation different from that of the preceding sibling. In addition to increasing numbers of interactions, the family changes in many other ways as each child is added. Dad and Mom have changed as parents: They have modified their expectations, added skills, and increased or decreased tolerances. The number of formal and informal roles within the family has increased, social expectations have changed, and financial needs (and possibly income) are different. The impact of these changes on the family is what we see when we look at birth-order differences.

Because of the subtleties of communication within families, the character traits associated with birth positions are remarkably consistent over time. This is true in spite of changes that take place within families. A number of studies published by Drs. Margaret

Hoopes and James Harper reflect this fact, as described in *Birth Order Roles and Sibling Patterns in Individual and Family Therapy:*

> Although parents and other family members are explicit about some of their expectations for each sibling, they also communicate their expectations at the implicit level. In spite of the lack of explicit communication, role assignments are functional in that they define the child's responsibilities in the system. Children respond to messages received and, while serving the family, learn to meet their individual needs through the family and specific family members. Thus, the assignment and acceptance of the role occur at the interface of system and individual needs.
>
> The outward behavior of the role may change as the child passes through various stages of development and develops a personality commensurate with his or her capabilities and physical, mental and emotional experiences. The basic responsibilities do not change, however.[2]

As we explore each sibling position, remember that each family member impacts all of the others. Pay attention to your own position and also to the positions of your siblings and parents. Unless specifically noted, the traits apply similarly to either males or females.

The Firstborn

Most firstborn kids have a fairly tough time of it. Being new to their responsibility, parents tend to have high expectations. By the time children number two and number three come along, Mom and Dad have faced a little reality, and child number one has taken the edge off of their idealism. Nevertheless, since everything child number one does is a "first" for the parents, their expectations for him or her tend to remain fairly high. One father of four sons humorously shared this insight: "My first son walked when he was nine months old, mainly because I *made* him walk! We practiced every day for weeks— I'm surprised he isn't bow-legged. My second son

2. M. M. Hoopes and J. M. Harper. *Birth Order Roles and Sibling Patterns in Individual and Family Therapy* (Rockville, Md.: Aspen Publishers Inc., 1987), 26.

didn't walk until he was fourteen months old. That's because I didn't care if he ever walked; I already had one that walked."

Because it is natural for children to try to meet the expectations of their parents, firstborn kids end up with some fairly consistent behavior patterns. Firstborns often develop into a type of "assistant parent." Given the responsibility of being an example to the younger children, most firstborns fall into a pattern of making decisions, giving orders, teaching, protecting, and correcting misbehavior. They are leaders. Oldest siblings tend to have fairly high expectations for themselves and are frequently self-critical.

Firstborns tend to develop two sets of personality traits, being either compliant and responsible or independent, assertive, and strong willed.

Compliant and responsible firstborns may become Dad and Mom's "appendage," having clear authority over younger siblings and carrying out orders. Although they hold a position of leadership, these children initiate very little. They get rewarded for their leadership and become very successful at it in the home.

Outside of the home, these individuals are viewed as ideal students and employees. They have a strong need for approval, especially from authority figures. As a result, they are cooperative, reliable, conscientious, and appreciated by their leaders and mentors.

Compliant firstborns also tend to be easily manipulated. Assertiveness doesn't come easily and they have a natural desire to please others, so it is fairly easy for others to take advantage of them. As children they are given responsibility for siblings; as adults they continue the pattern by taking responsibility for others. They are the "doormats" around the office or the overcommitted church members. When someone says, "I'd like you to . . ." they automatically respond, "Sure!" Even when overcommitted and overloaded, it is extremely difficult for these compliant firstborns to disappoint others by backing out and slowing down. Frequently they become quietly resentful and bitter.

Some compliant firstborns are unable to please their parents, typically because of unrealistic expectations placed on them. When positive reinforcement is consistently missing in the home, the compliant firstborn often becomes the "frustrated failure." When this child can't measure up to his parents' standards, instead of working harder to please others, he or she gives up. As an adult this individual is passive, unmotivated, and chronically self-defeating. Rather than risk repeated failure and rejection, this person learns to avoid the attempt.

The second personality common to firstborns is that of the "driver," who is independent, assertive, and strong willed. Rather than waiting for leadership to be handed over to him or her, this child has learned to take it. With confidence and initiative, this child organizes the others on the playground. Directing and controlling others seem to come naturally.

As adults these individuals tend to be high achievers, extremely productive and energetic, outperforming their peers. They are competitive and take pride in being able to do more in less time than anyone else.

While assertive firstborns are very successful professionally, they typically neglect relationships on their way to the top. Their need for control and focus on performance often make them difficult to become close to emotionally.

Regardless of which personality traits they display, it generally feels natural for firstborns to have expectations placed on them. Firstborns tend to be more perfectionistic than their siblings and are more apt to view their world in terms of black and white. Therefore, firstborn children tend to be fairly inflexible when it comes to rules. Definitions of right and wrong, and good and bad, appear more distinct for these people, and they are often intent on having others comply with their interpretation of the rules. Whether compliant appendages or drivers, because of their unique position in the family most firstborns will always see authority as an interpersonal issue.

A disproportionate number of firstborns are found in professions that reward perfectionism and attention to details: accountants, scientists, doctors, and attorneys. Of the first twenty-three astronauts in the U.S. space program, twenty-one were firstborn or only children! (A high percentage of only children are found in these same professions. We'll discuss them later.)

In a marriage relationship, firstborns tend to have a strong need for and expectation of control. They act self-assured even when they may feel insecure. Firstborns typically have difficulty accepting criticism from their spouses. The strengths and difficulties of the firstborn will affect a marriage in a number of ways. Many of these will depend on the personality (and birth order) of their partner.

If you are a firstborn, you would do well to lower the expectations you have for yourself. By performing less and relaxing more, you will find that your relationships naturally deepen. Unfortunately, learning to slow down and play is a hard lesson for firstborns to learn.

The Lastborn

As the firstborn has the familiar role of leader, the role most familiar to lastborns is that of follower. The youngest child is typically accustomed to being cared for, watched over, and provided for by siblings as well as parents. Lastborns can usually be characterized as performers or tagalongs.

A performer is a child who grows up being coddled, catered to, and focused on by the rest of the family. Mom and Dad may be overjoyed with "little dumpling" and focus a great deal of attention on him or her. The other kids will generally follow the parents' lead, and the little one ends up being "on stage" most of the time. Cute antics are rewarded and encouraged by attention, laughter, and discussion. As the center of attention for the family, this member develops into a "performer." He learns to be very aware of people's responses to him and often becomes a very effective manipulator. This child has the tendency to be spoiled, moody, and impulsive. Charming, personable, and affectionate, lastborn children often make very effective sales representatives.

A lastborn child who grows up being minimized—ignored, or not taken seriously—may become a tagalong. Mom and Dad may be very busy at this stage in their life, with their attention divided among the other children, jobs, hobbies, and social life. In this case, "little tagalong" may end up with whatever energy and attention is left over.

For this child, the familiar role is that of being directed and led. These individuals grow up with a strong emotional dependence on others. Decision-making is often difficult. They tend to be agreeable and conforming, tagging along with anybody's program. They are most comfortable in settings where someone else in charge will give them clear direction.

In either one of these scenarios, youngest children are not treated as peers by anyone in the family. They are not given as much responsibility and less maturity is expected of them. Parental demands are focused elsewhere.

Lastborns tend to be more carefree and less prone to worry than their siblings. They have less need to be in control and have less concern about detail. They tend to be more social and have a high need for the attention of others. Because of their thirst for attention, they respond well to encouragement. A pep talk and a few "attaboys" motivate lastborns to achieve, though their efforts may be short-lived if the praise drops off.

Most lastborns dream of greatness, though this may be their private secret. This may be anything from swimming the Pacific to becoming president. This secret desire for grandeur is probably a response to watching older siblings do everything first while being told they're not big enough yet.

In a marriage relationship, lastborns tend to bring out the dominant side of their partners, who are often firstborns. The lastborn personality seems to invite a parenting response from others, though this may not be obvious before marriage. The spontaneous, vivacious, playful characteristics of a lastborn that are attractive in courtship are also the impulsive, temperamental, irresponsible traits that drive a firstborn spouse crazy.

If you are a lastborn, beware of your tendency toward self-centeredness. Try to find something benevolent to do for which you will not be recognized. Each day, look for someone's need you can meet secretly. Learn to enjoy the inner sense of value that God gives in secret.

The Middle Child

The designation of "middle child" applies to anyone born between the first and last child. In a family of three children, that means the secondborn. If there are five kids, it means second-, third-, and fourthborn. The middle child is the one with the fewest photos in the family album, and the most hand-me-down clothes in his wardrobe. Like a wheel that doesn't squeak, middle children are easy to overlook.

While the parents' responses to the oldest and the youngest kids tend to be fairly predictable, responses to middle children vary. The family's response to them is less predictable, so middleborn children often have no automatic role that is given them on the basis of their birth order. Where middle children "fit" will tend to be influenced primarily by other factors, particularly the number, ages, and gender of their siblings.

Personality development of the middle child is probably most strongly determined by the personality of the older sibling. Because the middle position has no inherent uniqueness, these children need to seek out a special identity within the family. Since the younger siblings will probably lose the competition for whichever spot the firstborn has chosen, their identity will be developed by watching the older sibling and taking off in other directions.

As with the other birth-order positions, this personality generally takes one of two forms. Some middle children become competitors in order to earn a place of recognition in the family, while others are invisible children, unable to gain recognition.

The competitor feels he or she has to earn a place of recognition within the family. Generally unable to successfully take over the role occupied by the firstborn sibling, this child develops other areas around which to develop an identity. If the firstborn has found an area in which to excel, the second child will typically develop skills in some opposite area:

> If the firstborn is rebellious, the secondborn will be compliant.
> If the firstborn is an athlete, the secondborn will be a scholar or musician.

If the the firstborn is social and outgoing, the secondborn will
be quiet and introspective.
If the firstborn is structured and organized, the secondborn will
be random and spontaneous.

Although the combinations are endless, the pattern is typical.

The invisible child cannot find a place of recognition within the
family. For a number of possible reasons, he or she is not rewarded
for success in any particular area. This is the child who eventually
gives up on success, because whatever attempts he has made have
met with frustration and failure. While this may happen to children
in other sibling positions, the oldest and youngest have other factors inherent in their positions that tend to modify their responses
to failure. While the oldest child may become the rebel and the
youngest may become the clown, the middle child often becomes
the loser.

Whatever form their personalities take, middle children are usually the members who function most independently of the family.
They tend to be more emotionally distant than other family members and their primary source of emotional support generally comes
from outside the family, usually from their peers.

One experience universal to all middle children is that of having
a comfortable role taken from them. All middle children were at
one point the lastborn. The attention naturally showered on the
baby of the family once belonged to them, until younger brother
or sister came along. Having little choice but to adapt to the new
birth order, middle children learn to adjust.

Sandwiched between the personalities of their older and younger
siblings, adaptation and compromise are requirements for survival
for middle children, who typically develop numerous skills in negotiating and mediating. As adults they are frequently in the middle
of someone else's conflict, trying to bring opposing sides together.
In their helpfulness to others, middle children may lose track of
their own values and preferences and wind up not having a clear
sense of their own identity.

In a marriage relationship, middle children can be hard to get
close to emotionally. Since these people naturally adapt to those

around them, it may be difficult to determine what middle children actually feel. Uncomfortable with conflict or confrontation, they may withdraw in silence rather than face these problems directly. Middle children may passively choose to live with hurt and offense rather than "make waves." In contrast to the firstborn child, the middle child is the least likely of the siblings to have a need for control.

If you are a middleborn child, you would do well to pay more attention to your own values, beliefs, and opinions. It is easy for middle children to compromise and adapt to others until they seem to have no views or feelings of their own. While expressing these directly may be uncomfortable, you will almost always find your relationships improving as a result of your openness and transparency.

The Only Child

Only children often become an interesting blend of traits common in both the firstborn and lastborn children. Their behavior, perspectives, and reactions are typical of firstborns, but emotionally they are very similar to lastborn children.

Since their parents' expectations are usually high, as they are for firstborn children, only children tend to be performers and high achievers. They have a tendency toward perfectionism, and their verbal skills are usually well above average. These are all characteristics shared with firstborn children.

The other side of the coin is that only children spend their formative years being the "main event" of their parents' lives. Similar to the experience of many lastborn children, being the focus of attention often becomes part of the only child's expectations of life.

The personality of the only child may take one of two general directions, that of treasured only or structured only, depending on the circumstances of birth.

The treasured only is the only child whose parents had a desire for more children but for one reason or another were able to have only one. Poor health or other medical problems, several miscarriages or stillbirths, or perhaps just growing older may be factors that prevented the parents from having other children. Whatever the reason, the only child born to this couple tends to become the center of the universe for these parents. This focus of attention, time, and energy often results in a child who may have difficulty sharing the spotlight with others and who is seen as being spoiled or self-centered.

The structured only is the child whose parents had only one child because they chose to have only one child. They planned their family this way and stuck to their plan. Perhaps they decided that multiple children required too much work or energy, or perhaps their priorities were elsewhere. In any case, these parents are generally well-organized, self-disciplined planners. The household tends to be a fairly structured, disciplined home and the child develops in accord with this atmosphere. This family often expects the child to be a miniature adult, so the child tends to behave maturely but feels uncomfortable among peers.

In either case, the only child grows up relating closely with adults rather than other children. He or she may not learn to interact comfortably with peers, though feeling very at ease with authority figures. Only children tend to be less spontaneous and playful than other children, and while their verbal skills are usually very good, they may be the least talkative in a group. They often have difficulty developing close relationships and frequently describe themselves as lonely. As these discomforts are generally kept inside, only children appear to cope fairly well in life. As adults they frequently appear very confident and self-assured in social situations, but inwardly they feel vaguely uncomfortable, insecure, and ill at ease.

In a marriage relationship, only children often struggle to cope with the idiosyncrasies of another personality. Normal mood changes in their partners are especially frustrating and confusing for only children. While they may deeply love, care for, and enjoy their partners, only children tend to be most comfortable when alone.

If you are an only child, you will gain a great deal by paying close attention to your self-talk. You are probably unaware of the critical and demeaning statements you make to yourself. Only children typically need to practice honest, encouraging, positive self-evaluation. Find several trustworthy friends with whom you can share what you are learning on this journey into your family's past.

Twins

The placement of twins in birth order is more complex than that of single-birth children. Some studies indicate that each twin develops the characteristics typical of the birth order position to which he or she is born. For example, in twins born to a family with an older sibling, the older twin will develop characteristics of a second-born and the younger twin will take on the role of a thirdborn sibling. Most twins know which of them was born first. This may indicate the family's tendency to respond to them according to their birth order and reinforce these characteristics.

Nevertheless, the traits I've observed in twin siblings most often seem to stem from factors other than set patterns in birth order. For instance, if one twin is disabled in some way, that child will tend to develop as a lastborn due to the attention he or she receives, regardless of birth order. The same would be true of a twin girl born to a family of all boys, or the only boy in a family of girls.

Twins as a unit generally have a very special place in the family—twins are special, and they usually know it. In many families twins are treated as lastborns, regardless of when they arrive.

Variables Affecting Birth Order

It would be nice if understanding the effects of birth order were as simple as counting siblings and looking at a chart. It's a little more complex than that. The effect of your birth order is actually a reflection of how your family interacts with you. Many factors can affect how a family responds to each child.

Handicapped Siblings

A child who is handicapped and therefore requires extra care and attention will affect each of the other family members in some way. A firstborn mentally retarded son may cause the secondborn sister to function as a typical oldest child because family expectations will be higher for her. A middle child born physically disabled may cause the lastborn child to develop a nurturant, care-taking personality which is unusual for lastborns. Most commonly, the family will interact with a handicapped child as though that child were the youngest; that special child often becomes the lastborn regardless of birth order.

Six Years or More between Subsequent Siblings

When a child is born after a childless gap of six years or more, the birth order usually starts over. As an example, let's say that Bobby is six years old when little sister Sally is born. Bobby, now in school full time, is beginning to make friends and look to authority figures outside of the family. Because of their age difference, he will probably never spend much time with Sally. Because of Bobby's growing independence, Mom and Dad will probably have more time available to spend with Sally than they would if Bobby were younger. They've developed a whole new set of expectations over the last six years with which Sally will be raised. Sally will probably grow up in an environment very similar to that of most firstborns and therefore will tend to develop traits typical of firstborn children.

Parents' Birth Order

Parents have unique family histories of their own that affect their perceptions and reactions. Since birth order is a part of their background, responses to their children are influenced by their own parents' responses. A woman who grew up as the eldest of six children with five younger brothers developed certain expectations regarding that role of firstborn. If she has a family of four sons and a secondborn daughter, she might expect her only same-sex child to fulfill the roles and duties of a firstborn, as she had, regardless of her daughter's birth order. Those expectations become a variable that influences the effect of birth order in this new generation.

Parenting Style

Naturally, a parent's overall approach to parenting will affect the response of the child. This fact is key to understanding birth order. Some parents approach their parenting role with overbearing demands, unrealistic expectations, or consistent criticism. Such a parenting style can turn a conscientious firstborn into a rebel leader— or a spontaneous mascot into a passive scapegoat.

Premature Death of a Sibling

The death of a child has been called the ultimate bereavement. A family's grieving and mourning will alter the family's functioning in many ways—some subtle, some obvious. The death of a child also changes the birth order within the family. Expectations of parents and siblings change and each family member reacts accordingly.

When a social, assertive firstborn dies, the secondborn may give up familiar passive traits and take over the leader's role. The parents may redirect their expectations and aspirations for the deceased sibling to another child with similar characteristics or of the same gender. A child born into the family during the charged time of grief following such a loss would experience a unique atmosphere and be set apart because of it. If the grieving is never discussed or resolved, that child may carry an emotional heaviness and sense of depression that he or she doesn't understand. If family members carry feelings of guilt associated with the death, that guilt may be unconsciously communicated to, or projected onto, the new child without anyone's conscious awareness. All of these potential effects, as well as countless others, will vary from family to family.

Ethnic Background

Often a family's national heritage will affect the expectations of birth order. Many nationalities, notably Mideastern and some European cultures, place a heavy emphasis and responsibility on the male children regardless of their birth order. In such a family it's common to find the eldest boy functioning as a firstborn even if he may have several older sisters. Since he is expected to display traits characteristic of firstborns, his character develops accordingly.

Divorce, Separation, Death, or Disability of Parents

Formal family roles tend to change radically in the aftermath of loss due to divorce, separation, death, or disability of parents. As a parent is taken out of a familiar role, the tasks involved in that role are taken over by other family members. When Mother dies, the secondborn daughter may assume the caring, nurturant role with her siblings and function as a firstborn, even though she has an older brother.

Gender Distribution

If one daughter is born to a family with many boys or if one son has many sisters, it is not uncommon for that unique sibling to function as a lastborn no matter where he or she falls in the sibling lineup. The exception to this may be when the only boy or girl is firstborn. In this case, this oldest sibling may function as an "ultra" firstborn, playing the nurturant, care-taking role to the younger siblings.

Adopted Children

An adopted child tends to be treated as a lastborn regardless of birth order. The reasons for this are similar to those explained for a child with some unique characteristic such as physical or mental handicap, or being the only female sibling.

Before you continue on to the next leg of your journey, take some time to write in your notebook any new information or insights you have acquired up to this point. As you review previous chapters, look for consistent themes and patterns in your past—especially as they relate directly to your life today. Begin to think about the significant people in your life. How do they (and their pasts) impact on you?

Your Personal Family Voyage

1. How has your birth order been a benefit to you in each of the following?

   Your close relationships

   Your occupation

   Your life goals

2. In what ways do you think your birth order has resulted in difficulties for you?

3. How did your parents' birth orders affect their approach to parenting? Was the impact on you positive or negative?

4. Name any of your own personality traits that you can attribute to your birth order. Which of these characteristics do you value most? Why? Which of these traits would you like to change?

5. After completing this book, use the steps outlined in the last chapter to structure a specific plan to change one of these characteristics.

7

So Who's Normal?

Many people seem to believe
that a healthy, functional family
is one free of problems.
Since we are all imperfect,
fallen human beings,
every family has difficulties.

W hat is normal?" As a family therapist I hear this question often. It's one of those difficult questions we therapists tend to politely avoid by turning it in a different direction. Why is this particular query so thorny? Because the term *normal* assumes a comparison to most other families and frankly, a significant proportion of families in our society have serious problems, many of which are denied. Almost anyone can feel better about his or her situation by finding someone whose problems are more serious. But feeling better about our own struggles by denying or minimizing them will prevent their resolution. Since the person inquiring is almost always looking for a way to evaluate his own situation, he is actually asking the wrong question.

So what is the right question? Let's use the term *functional* instead of *normal*, to form a more appropriate question: What characterizes a functional family? *Functional* and *dysfunctional* are not comparative terms. They are terms that describe how successfully something achieves a goal. A functional family is literally one that "works"; a dysfunctional family is one that doesn't work.

What Makes a Family Work?

Since the functional family is one that works, we need to begin by understanding the "job" of a family. A family has three main tasks, each of which involves meeting the needs of the family members, especially the most vulnerable, the children. Needs can be separated into three categories: maintenance, nurturance, and guidance.

Maintenance needs are those things needed for survival—food, shelter, and physical safety. If your family met your maintenance needs as a child, when you were hungry you were given food. When your outgrew your clothes, someone would replace them. When you were tired, you were provided a place to sleep. Such provisions make children feel that someone stronger is watching out for them. This task of the family gives children a sense of safety and stability and provides a context for developing trust.

Nurturance needs are the basic emotional requirements of affirmation, encouragement, and affection. If a family is meeting the children's nurturance needs, the children are praised for accomplishing tasks and are hugged and reassured when frightened. Nurturance means that children have people to laugh with, cry with, be honest with, and belong to. This task of the family gives children a sense of self-worth, love, and dignity.

Guidance needs involve preparation for adaptation to the outside world—training, role modeling, and educating. When children fail at a task, they are taught a better way. When they ask a question, they receive an answer. When they attempt something new, they are affirmed for their risk. Guidance involves teaching ethics, manners, and skills as well as the management of emotions and behavior. Moral and spiritual values are also a part of guidance. This task of the family gives children a sense of self-confidence and self-reliance. It provides children with a context for independence, courage, and success.

Resolving Problems

No parent can be completely affirming at all times or be a perfect role model in all aspects of life. No one is able to totally prepare children for all that life will bring them. Because of these human shortcomings, and because each of us grew up with certain needs that were not met by our families at least part of the time, the difference between functional and dysfunctional families is largely a matter of degree. Most families have both functional and dysfunctional aspects. Some families are primarily dysfunctional; some are primarily functional.

Many people seem to believe that a healthy, functional family is one free of problems. Since we are all imperfect, fallen human beings, every family has difficulties. Actually, a family that believes it is without problems is a family whose primary dysfunction is denial.

A healthy family is not measured by the absence of struggles but by its ability to resolve problems in the majority of cases. Genuine resolution does not leave a residue of bitterness but involves solutions that consider the needs and feelings of each family member.

In a functional family, Dad and Mom can discuss their dissatisfaction and frustration without screaming at or blaming each other. They can negotiate and make changes to improve their relationship. They can interact with their children about those changes, and the children can express their feelings and opinions as well. This model of communication by the parents is reflected in the children, and the family becomes a safe place to:

Express honest feelings and desires.
Be heard and respected in spite of disagreement.
Listen to others as significant individuals.

In a functional family, though this type of respectful interaction may not take place 100 percent of the time, it is the norm. The familiar pattern in a healthy family is mutual respect. Unresolved problems are the exception rather than the rule. While it may not be perfect, a functional family works as it should.

In a healthy family the child's basic needs are met in the majority of situations. The child in this home grows up with a sense that he or she is important. This child develops an internal sense of security and trust as well as a perspective that the world is basically a safe, though imperfect, place to live. With this inner sense of security there is less need to seek security through external sources such as chemicals, relationships, and behaviors.

When It Doesn't Work

In a dysfunctional family, certain needs of the child go unmet in the majority of situations. Basic needs for safety, nurturance, or guidance must be met by the children themselves in whatever way they can. In essence, a dysfunctional family is one that doesn't work. Most dysfunctional families will have one or more of the following characteristics.

Substance abuse by one or both parents. Use of chemicals—alcohol, narcotics, marijuana, or prescription drugs—to alter perceptions or moods.

Psychological or emotional disturbance of one or more family members. These members who suffer from chronic depression, schizophrenia, compulsivity, manic depression, or another disorder, become the hub around which the family functions.

Rigid or harsh parenting style. Unreasonable demands and expectations, dogmatic rules, or authoritarianism. These are combined with an absence of affirmation and a focus on the negative characteristics of the child.

Constant conflict. Consistent emotional tension and unrest within the home. Verbal abuse between parents and among family members.

Physical abuse. Excessive physical discipline and/or punishment administered in anger. Anger-management problems among family members.

Sexual abuse. Pornography in the home; inappropriate exposure of children to sexually stimulating material; sexual behavior toward children; seductive behavior patterns among family members.

Emotional incest. Unhealthy bonds between parent and child; emotional dependence of a parent on a child; a parent consulting or confiding in a child about marital problems; a child used as mediator in conflict between parents.

The result of these dysfunctions is a deficit within the family in one or more of the following areas.

Neglect. The child's physical and/or emotional needs are ignored. Children are treated as intrusions into the lives of adults, as though they were consistently in the way. A sense of being unprotected, unimportant, and devalued is communicated to the children.

Chaos. There is little or no guidance or leadership for the child. Parents are unavailable either physically or emotionally. Boundaries are inconsistent or nonexistent. Life for the child seems out of control.

Abuse. Children are disrespected and treated poorly and inappropriately. Abuse may be physical, sexual, emotional, or verbal. The children experience ongoing fear, insecurity, and shame.

Denial. Parents hide or cover up reality, pretending that problems don't exist; the children follow their lead. Denial distorts the children's perception of reality, as they learn to distrust their senses and observations.

Children in a dysfunctional family learn to pay close attention to the stability—or instability—of the family system. They are aware when Mom starts drinking or when Dad's getting angry. When they perceive the familiar cues, they respond with familiar defensive behaviors that will stabilize the situation. These behaviors tend to be amplifications of the informal family roles discussed in chapter 4.

Control becomes extremely important within the dysfunctional home. When Dad beats Mom or Mom threatens divorce, each member attempts to control his or her world in some way in order to survive emotionally. Each looks to the others for clues as to how to behave. Life often becomes a series of reactions to the environment. Once they reach adulthood, people who grew up in a family like this often have a powerful need to remain in control of any situation. Lack of control can cause panic.

Dysfunctional homes produce individuals who spend much of their energy searching for what they perceive to be "normal." They constantly compare themselves to others in hopes of being "okay." In his book *Unfinished Business*, Charles Sell describes this dilemma well:

> There is a simple yet complex explanation for this obsessive grop-
> ing for what is normal. In a more normal home, a person learns what

works in human relationships—a child who knew how it felt to be hugged knows hugging is okay; a boy who saw a certain amount of arguing between his parents knows that normal homes can tolerate a certain amount of fighting without people getting hurt or feeling grossly ashamed.

In a "normal" family, Mom might lose her cool because her teenage daughter left dishes in the sink. No harm done; the daughter goes away muttering, "Boy, was she mad," knowing Mom still loves her. But suppose a daughter grew up in a home where Mom beat her for trivial mistakes. When she becomes a mom, she could be scared to death by a normal display of anger toward her child. An adult child describes the typical confusion:

"Growing up in a home that was dominated by conflict, it's difficult to know how much conflict to expect in my own marriage. When my dad drank, my mom and dad fought for the whole evening. When I got married I was determined we would never fight. It took me a long time to realize I was really afraid of conflict and that to be a good husband and parent you have to face it, not run from it. Not really knowing what to expect of myself or others has created a lot of problems for me. I overreact to others' faults, especially my children's, because I have a hard time tolerating faults. Along with massive doses of frustration, I feel guilty much of the time because I'm never sure I'm doing the right thing."[1]

One of the most profound effects of a dysfunctional family is that the family patterns are typically projected onto God. Individuals who did not have authority figures they could trust will have difficulty trusting God. Many sincere Christians can intellectually understand the trustworthiness of God but cannot emotionally rest in him. They have a deep inner need to remain in control as though God may abandon them. Worry and anxiety over situations beyond their control can feel overwhelming. Their guilt and shame over their distrust only amplifies the tension. The struggle between what they know biblically and what they feel emotionally causes untold turmoil for many Christians.

1. Charles Sell. *Unfinished Business* (Portland, Oreg.: Multnomah Press, 1989), 55–56.

Adult Children

Adult child is a term used to describe an adult who grew up in a dysfunctional home. As mentioned earlier, the dysfunction may have stemmed from a parent's alcoholism, mental illness, abusive temper, or even ignorance. Whatever the cause, the adult child is a person who had a significant need or needs that went unmet in the majority of cases during childhood. He or she may have grown and matured physically and mentally, but emotionally is still an insecure, fearful, reactive child. Many distorted emotional patterns from childhood remain intact; though at times these are well disguised, they often wreak havoc in adult relationships.

Pete's Story

Pete is fairly typical of hundreds of adult children I've worked with. The specifics of the family of origin may differ somewhat, but the patterns he carries are very familiar. Pete came to my office initially to deal with job-related stress management problems as well as with some relational difficulties.

Pete was a compulsive people-pleaser. For as long as he could remember, it had been extremely important that others like and accept him. He was very sensitive to criticism, often growing defensive or withdrawing in silence when corrected. If someone was angry or disappointed with Pete, he would obsessively go to almost any length to alter that person's perception of him.

Pete was also a perfectionist. Since he needed everyone to be pleased with everything he did, no detail was too small to overlook. This meant that every task involved great time and effort and many tasks went uncompleted; others were never begun. When friends and co-workers grew frustrated with Pete, his emotional tension only increased.

Emotional expression was almost impossible for Pete. Through the years he'd put so much of his energy and attention into making others feel good about him that he generally had no idea what his true feelings were.

Pete found himself constantly performing, trying to be whatever anyone seemed to want him to be. At thirty-two, he had no idea who he was. His values, preferences, and priorities had been adjusted and adapted so many times that he had lost track of them. His life became little more than a reflection of whomever he was with.

This was not Pete's first attempt at changing his behavior. He'd been in counseling on three other occasions and had read dozens of books. His success was always marginal and short-lived. Never had Pete made a connection between his current dissatisfaction and the "emotional training" he had received at home.

Pete's family history is a familiar story for many adult children. His father was an alcoholic—a fact never discussed by anyone in the family. When Dad would come home drunk and pass out on the floor, Mom would cover him with a blanket and tell the children that he was too tired to go to bed. Even as a child Pete could sense that this wasn't the case, but as with most children, he accepted his mother's explanation and dismissed his perceptions as wrong. When Dad exploded in a drunken rage, venting his fury on various family members, Mom explained that he wasn't feeling well, end of discussion. Taught not to speak of these private things—the family secret—Pete told no one outside the family of the turmoil.

Pete grew up having no relationship with his father, except to avoid or appease him. Pete's needs for friendship, guidance, and nurturance were never met by his father, and his mother was usually too fearful or exhausted to be emotionally available.

Until Pete began school, this situation was "normal" to him. Pete knew nothing else and assumed all families were like his. As he began to make and visit new friends, his perspective began to change. He discovered that Billy's dad never hit his mom or vomited on the floor. Jeff's parents read stories to him and sometimes went camping in the summer. Joey's family went to ball games together. At this point Pete made a very subtle decision.

He never verbalized it to anyone, but it changed his view of everything and everyone profoundly. Pete decided that whatever Billy's, Jeff's, and Joey's families were, his should be also, so he began to imitate them as best he could. He became even more secretive about the reality of his family and began his life of performing for others.

But Pete didn't realize that what he observed in his friends' homes was also a performance. Since he was "company" when he visited in their homes, these families were on their best behavior. From his young perspective he concluded that they never fought, argued, disagreed, or experienced anger in any way. They were always smiling, pleasant, and warm. His immature conclusion was to idealize every family, except his own. He saw every child's needs being fully met, except his. He separated families into two categories: good and bad. He believed that the vast majority of families fell into the "good" category. He was among the very few who had "bad" families. He began working very hard to be sure that no one discovered how radically "different" he was.

These perceptions set in motion several patterns for Pete that would persist well into adulthood. He saw himself as an outsider looking in. "Normal" life was being lived by others, and he was trying to imitate it. He tried to guess what normal was, and then he tried to reproduce it in his own life. Since Pete had no one to help him evaluate his perceptions, they went uncorrected. Of course, these patterns developed gradually and subtly, often without his conscious awareness. Any awareness of these struggles he may have had as a child was forgotten long ago.

Pete's initial discovery in therapy was similar to that of many adult children. He began to see that the patterns he attempted to leave behind had fostered powerful distortions in his experience of life. He'd entered adulthood with a sense of insecurity and inadequacy. All his life he'd attempted to achieve a sense of security through his behavior. His search for external security had resulted in the compulsive performing that had defined his life for more than two decades.

As a result of his family voyage, I suggested that Pete join a Christian support group for adult children. This became the path of genuine recovery for Pete. These loving, supportive people understood his struggles; they were actively resolving these issues in their own lives.

Though he was a Christian, Pete never realized the role of his heavenly Father in meeting the needs left unmet by his earthly father. He discovered that God has modeled a healthy relationship for him. God spoke clearly and shared his feelings openly. He chose to become vulnerable and invites us to share emotionally with him. He listens attentively and responds to us. He demonstrates his faithfulness and invites us to trust him.

Through loving confrontation and support of the group, Pete learned to accept the inner security available through his relationship with Christ. It required some risk on his part and a willingness to trust others as well as God. It was a slow process for Pete, and in many ways it is still continuing.

Characteristics

Through his support group, Pete found that although his story is unique, his struggles are very common. Many of the most common characteristics found in adult children of dysfunctional families are given below.

Self-doubt, self-criticism, self-blame. As children, we tend to blame ourselves for what happens to us and around us. This results in low self-esteem as adults. Low self-esteem is a deep sense that something is basically wrong with us, that we are defective and inadequate in some way. Adult children have learned to hide these feelings from others (and even from themselves) through many defenses. The most common methods of hiding these feelings of worthlessness are:

Perfectionism, an attempt to prove worthiness
Being critical, an attempt to show others as worthless
Caretaking, an attempt to earn the love and approval of others
Emotional control, an attempt to keep feelings from surfacing

Passivity. Adult children experience a sense of shame when they stand up for themselves in any way. Assertiveness can feel wrong, even sinful. Many adult children give in to the demands of others even when doing so is detrimental to themselves.

Emotional dependence. Adult children are often terrified of failure or rejection of any kind. This fear can keep them from entering new situations that are healthy and rewarding. They also remain in jobs, relationships, and other situations that are harmful to them to avoid the possibility of feeling isolated and abandoned.

Overresponsibility or underresponsibility. An overresponsible individual focuses attention on the problems and responsibilities of others. The irresponsible person avoids dealing with any problems at all. In either case, the adult child avoids self-examination and painful emotions.

Victimization. Helplessness is a familiar feeling in a dysfunctional home. Frequently adult children will develop a perspective on life that perpetuates this sense of impotence. They are often attracted to other "victims" out of a sense of identification or pity.

Need for approval. Adult children will go to great lengths to make people like them. This need for approval can result in a sense of loyalty that may go far beyond reasonable limits, even to the point of enduring ongoing personal abuse.

Oversensitivity to criticism. Because adult children tend to be very self-critical, their tolerance for criticism from others is low. This may lead to overreactions when confronted or corrected. Angry outbursts, severe hurt, or withdrawal may be out of proportion to the criticism received.

Fear of intimacy or emotional closeness. Adult children live with a vague sense of being different from others. This results in anxiety about being emotionally open or vulnerable. The adult child will naturally anticipate rejection. A common defense is to keep relationships superficial, even avoiding all social involvement with others. This is often most evident in relationships with perceived authority figures.

Repression, minimization, and denial of painful emotions. The adult child learned early in life that feelings aren't safe; to be vulnerable is to risk being hurt. Since there is a great deal of emotionally painful history in a dysfunctional family, that pain gets pushed aside, avoided, and ignored. It is not uncommon for the adult child to have completely blocked out the memory of large portions of childhood. Many adult children carry this pattern of repression into their present experience and cannot express emotions of any kind, and they have no clue as to why or how it is affecting their lives.

A need to be in control. Since dysfunctional families tend to be unpredictable and emotionally unstable, most adult children have a strong need to stay in control. Changes tend to cause intense anxiety for the adult child, especially when they are initiated by other people or external circumstances. The methods used to control others may vary from aggression to passivity, from subtle lies to tantrums.

Unmerited feelings of guilt. Dysfunctional families tend to project blame for problems onto their children. The children, in turn, accept this blame, especially when young. As a result, adult children feel shame for events and decisions over which they have no control and for problems they are powerless to solve.

Chronically unhealthy relationships. Adult children tend to be attracted to emotionally unavailable people with problems similar to the adult child's family of origin. Addiction, abuse, and neglect are often themes in a succession of partners. Adult children may feel uncomfortable and distant around healthy, caring people.

"Black-and-white" thinking. Adult children tend to have extreme views of the world. Situations, experiences, and people are viewed as either right or wrong, good or bad, wonderful or terrible. There is little room in their perspective for areas of gray or for a blending of qualities within the same person.[2]

2. For further study on adult children and their symptoms I recommend *Adult Children* by John and Linda Friel.

Looking for Artichokes

I have worked with many adult children as they have explored their pasts and begun to see the impact of their dysfunctional families. Initially, it is not unusual for them to experience anger, resentment, and even feelings of rage over what their families did or did not do for them. Assuming they do not deny these feelings or try to escape from them, eventually these feelings give way to a new perspective of their past.

A number of years ago I heard an illustration that beautifully depicts the recovery experience of many adult children of dysfunctional families:

Picture yourself going into a grocery store. You want to buy an artichoke for dinner. That's all, just an artichoke. You go through the produce section and don't see any artichokes. As you're looking, you start to get annoyed. You look all over the store and can't find a single artichoke anywhere. "Boy, that's irritating!" you think. "A store that looks as nice as this one *must* have some artichokes!"

You go to the counter and ask the cashier where to find the artichokes.

She responds, "I'm sorry, we don't carry artichokes here."

Now you're starting to get angry. You take out your money, place it in front of the cashier, and say, "Here's fifty dollars. That should be plenty for an artichoke! Please get me one."

Her response is the same: "I'm sorry, we don't have any artichokes in this store."

At this point you demand to speak to the manager. You tell the manager what you want but the response is still the same: "Sorry, no artichokes." You jump onto the counter, stomp your feet, scream, and make an absolute fool of yourself. Eventually you exhaust yourself with your tantrum.

At this point you are in a position to realize the truth: You can't get artichokes from a store that has no artichokes. Your anger is not a factor; your money is not a factor; the volume of your voice is not a factor. There are no artichokes here.

Now, once you've calmed down, you'll notice that across the street is another grocery store. They have artichokes on sale today, lots of 'em. You'll also notice if you take the time to look around, that the store you're in carries many quality products. Fresh meat, canned goods, bakery items. But no artichokes. By changing your focus just a little, you'll find that your needs can be met quite well by other options available to you. You will have to consider and explore those options, and you will have to accept the fact that not all options are under your control.

Let's apply this analogy to dysfunctional relationships. Let's say that your mother was not nurturing. Mothers are supposed to provide nurturance, but yours didn't. Perhaps her own mother had no nurturance to offer or model for her. She may have been scarred by her own history. As an adult you have some choices to make regarding this valid, unmet need in your life. Your options are:

1. Keep returning to Mother—in anger, in shame, or in repentance. Even if Mom is no longer living, you may blame her, ridicule her, or protect her in an attempt to get her to meet your need for nurturance. You may do it in person, in your imagination, or in your dreams. However you go about it, you may find that she is not and never was capable of offering you nurturance, and you can't fix that. The more you attempt to get her to do what she will not or cannot do, the more intense your frustration and anger will become.
2. Reject Mom altogether—assume that she's an evil person and worthless to you. Stay away from her; don't talk to her; punish her with your absence and your silence. In doing this, you are planting and watering a seed of bitterness within you that will bear fruit in many other areas of your life.
3. Change your view of Mom a little. Take a step back and try to see her as handicapped rather than evil. She probably has a number of good qualities that you missed in your pursuit of nurturance. What strengths have you gained from her? How has God used her to help you develop?

Now, look around you. Chances are God *has* placed in your life a number of people who are experts at nurturing. You may not have noticed them because you assumed that nurturance should come from Mom. When we focus rigidly on a particular goal, we often miss out on God's wonderful alternative provisions. In the analogy, the shopper goes without artichokes because of his anger at a particular store. Similarly, you may live without loving support and nurturance in spite of the presence of loving people around you.

God can meet our needs in many ways. He may not follow our program, but he *can* meet our needs. Jesus said it very clearly in Matthew 7:7–11:

> Ask, and it shall be given to you; seek, and you shall find; knock, and it shall be opened to you. For every one who asks receives, and he who seeks finds, and to him who knocks it shall be opened. Or what man is there among you, when his son shall ask him for a loaf, will he give him a stone? Or if he shall ask for a fish, he will not give him a snake, will he? If you then, being evil, know how to give good gifts to your children, how much more shall your Father who is in heaven give what is good to those who ask Him!

God often meets our needs through circumstances and people we don't expect. Unfortunately, sometimes our needs still go unmet because we are not willing to seek God's provision or accept his solutions.

Your Own History

Many adult children of dysfunctional families find their emotional needs overpowering at times. On your own family voyage you may find yourself feeling overwhelmed or perplexed by your strong emotions. If this is the case, I encourage you to find a professional family therapist with whom to share your concerns. Look for one who shares your spiritual values and priorities. Your pastor may be helpful in locating the right person.

Feel free to ask the counselor about his or her own background, education, and personal faith. If you are uncomfortable, do not feel obligated to continue with a therapist who is not appropriate for you. If you have difficulty locating a Christian family therapist in your area, you may want to call or write the American Association of Pastoral Counselors or the Christian Association for Psychological Studies, both listed in the Sources.

Your Personal Family Voyage

<u>1   2   3   4   5   6   7   8   9   10</u>
Need totally unmet   Need completely met

The scale above represents the ability of a family to meet the needs of its members. Using this scale, do the following:

1. Place an "M" on the scale to indicate how well your family of origin met your basic maintenance needs.

2. Place an "N" on the scale to indicate how well you feel your nurturance needs were met by your family.

3. Place a "G" on the scale to indicate how well your need for guidance was met by your family of origin.

4. If you believe that some of your basic needs were largely unmet, what were those specific needs? What impact do they have on you today?

5. How has your experience of confidence in your family influenced your ability to trust God?

6. If you could change history, what changes would you make in your family of origin?

7. What impact would these changes have on you today?

8. Make a list of people and situations that could potentially address the needs listed in question 4. In what ways could you begin allowing these to fulfill these areas of your life today?

8

Codependency and Compulsions
Fruit of the Dysfunctional Family Tree

Like so many other family traits,
codependency is passed
from generation to generation.
Codependent parents produce
codependent children.
Instead of modeling love as giving,
love becomes a distorted pattern
of manipulating, demanding,
earning, and receiving.
The child's perspective of this love is
"If I only work hard enough,
then I'll be lovable."

The most common products of a dysfunctional family of origin are codependent relationships and compulsive behaviors. These two are so closely intertwined that in many cases they are synonymous.

Codependency is a relatively new term that is being thrown around quite a bit these days. For many, its definition seems vague. For others, it sounds suspiciously like an excuse for selfishness. Codependency is sometimes defined as a tendency to have compulsively unhealthy relationships. While this is one feature of codependency, it is more complex than that.

Originally the term was used to describe the condition of spouses of alcoholics. These people had developed a living pattern that was not only unhealthy for themselves but actually promoted the alcoholism. They were obsessed with "fixing" their partners; without someone to rescue, they had no direction or purpose in life. Being emotionally dependent on their chemically dependent partners, they were "codependent."

Today we have a much broader understanding of this condition. The term *codependent* is used to describe an individual who is so preoccupied with others that his or her own life suffers or becomes unmanageable. Codependency is a futile attempt to deal with internals—fear, hurt, anger, insecurity—by trying to control externals—people, events, objects. For the codependent, unresolved issues and unmet needs from a dysfunctional past are played out in current situations.

Compulsion is an old, familiar term rooted in the verb *compel*. A compulsion is a behavior we feel compelled to perform, repeated behavior patterns that are extremely resistant to change even though they cause numerous personal difficulties. Symptoms of an internal, emotional struggle, compulsions may take a variety of forms:

Gambling, criticizing, excessive shopping, nail biting, arguing, excessive hand washing, and lying are some examples.

Characteristics of Codependency

Melody Beattie, in her excellent book *Codependent No More*, discusses the dilemma of describing specific symptoms common to codependents:

> Although two codependents might disagree on the definition of codependency, if they discuss the issues with each other, each will probably sense what the other person means. They will share ideas about things they have in common—things they do, think, feel, and say—that are characteristic of codependency. It is on these points— symptoms, problems, coping mechanisms, or reactions—that most definitions and recovery programs overlap and agree. These points dictate recovery. They are the things we need to recognize, accept, live with, deal with, struggle through, and frequently change.
>
> Before I list the things codependents tend to do, however, I will make an important point: Having these problems does not mean we're bad, defective, or inferior. Some of us learned these behaviors as children. Other people learned them later in life. We may have learned some of these things from our interpretation of religion. Some women were taught these behaviors were desirable feminine attributes. Wherever we learned to do these things, most of us learned our lessons well.
>
> Most of us started doing these things out of necessity to protect ourselves and meet our needs. We performed, felt, and thought these things to survive—emotionally, mentally, and sometimes physically. We tried to understand and cope with our complex worlds in the best ways. It is not always easy to live with normal, healthy people. It is particularly difficult to live with sick, disturbed, or troubled people. It is horrible having to live with a raving alcoholic. Many of us have been trying to cope with outrageous circumstances, and these efforts have been both admirable and heroic. We have done the best we could.
>
> However, these self-protective devices may have outgrown their usefulness. Sometimes the things we do to protect ourselves turn on us and hurt us. They become self-destructive. Many codependents are barely surviving, and most aren't getting their needs met. As

counselor Scott Egleston says, codependency is a way of getting needs met that doesn't get needs met. We've been doing the wrong things for the right reasons.[1]

Beattie's book includes a long list of characteristics typical of codependency and hundreds of specific traits common to codependent individuals. I've summarized in the following list the key issues cited in most of the research on codependency. These characteristics are typical of codependency. Each is a source of or a reflection of the need for control.

1. Discontentedness. The codependent lives with the sense that something is missing in his or her life. This chronic discontentment is the driving force behind much of his or her behavior.
2. Blame. The codependent consistently looks to others as a source for his or her own happiness. The resulting unmet expectations amplify discontentment. The codependent often feels like a victim and blames others for his or her circumstances.
3. Guilt. The codependent is inwardly self-critical and frequently feels guilty. Never feeling quite "good enough," he or she minimizes or rejects compliments or praise. Nevertheless he or she has a low tolerance for criticism and is defensive when corrected. The codependent attempts to bolster his or her low self-concept by helping others.
4. Overresponsibility. The codependent takes unreasonable responsibility for others and feels compelled to solve other people's problems. He or she is attracted to needy people and often feels empty without a problem to solve or someone to rescue.
5. Control. The codependent is consistently worried about and preoccupied with situations beyond his or her control. Control is a major motivation in the codependent's life, and he or she attempts to control others through manipulation, blame, guilt, helplessness, threats, coercion, or directives. The co-

dependent feels frustrated and angry when his or her attempts to control fail, and he or she in turn feels controlled by others.

6. Approval. The approval of others is very important to the codependent. He or she has a deep fear of rejection and abandonment and as a result says yes when meaning no, overcommits and neglects his or her own needs. The codependent may compromise his or her values and preferences to avoid disapproval.

7. Extremes. The codependent's lifestyle and relationships are a series of extremes, frequently involving other compulsions. He or she vacillates between love and hate, hoarding and spending, hot and cold, up and down. He or she may lack a sense of healthy balance in one or more life areas.

Personal Boundaries

Many of the symptoms of codependency—overresponsibility, need for approval, need for control, and living in extremes—can be clearly seen if we discuss codependency in terms of personal boundaries.

In chapter 3 we explored the concept of how a family's emotional boundaries can reflect its sense of identity. Families have boundaries—emotional fences—that control who has access to the "property." Individuals also have boundaries—limits to what they allow others to do to them or take from them. Most of us regularly interact with people who want more of us—our time, energy, abilities, stamina—than we wish to or realistically can give. Considering our values, priorities, and preferences, we need to set our boundaries, which means sometimes saying, "No, I can't give that to you." Obviously, people will be displeased with us at least some of the time.

It's very difficult for the codependent who is consistently striving for approval to say, "no"—to establish any consistent boundaries. The result is a chaotic swing between feelings of guilt and resentment. Here's how it typically works:

Let's say that I'm feeling satisfied with my level of commitments. I have a good balance among work, family time, and outside activities. I'm at a point of personal equilibrium; my amount of "emotional space" is comfortable. Now, someone steps up to me in church and says, "Roger, we need someone to teach our young marrieds class. There are some really troubled couples in there. Since you're a marriage counselor, you'd be the perfect person. Can you do it? They meet on Thursday nights."

This is a reasonable request made by a well-meaning individual. But since my life is in balance right now, taking on something new would mean upsetting that balance or letting go of a previous commitment. So I answer, "I'm sorry, I won't be able to do that."

At this point I have established and communicated a boundary. This request is for time and energy that I prefer not to give to this class. I picture this boundary as similar to a fence around me. This person has come up to the edge of the boundary.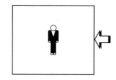

But let's say that this particular person is fairly assertive. He's not comfortable with the boundaries I've chosen. So he asks, "Why 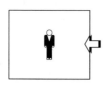 not? What are you doing Thursday nights?" This person isn't necessarily trying to be rude. He is convinced I'm the person to meet this particular need and he wants to help me solve whatever problems will keep me from doing it. (That type of manipulative control is also a symptom of co-dependency, but we'll just focus on me right now.) In essence he is trying to push past my boundary.

I reply, "Thursday evenings I spend with my kids." So I've clarified my boundary. To this he responds, "But these people really need you. Besides, Mr. Jones has seven children and he teaches five classes. Surely you can find a way to do it." Now he's pushing harder on my boundaries and trying to bring in guilt for leverage.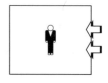

Let's say I give in at this point, not because I 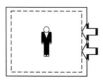 believe it's appropriate but to avoid a feeling of guilt or this person's disapproval. I sacrifice my balance, compromise my priorities, and allow my boundaries to be adjusted.

If this is the only time I allow this to happen, it's probably no big deal. But if I let this happen regularly, before long my boundaries will be getting pretty tight.

At this point, my life will be significantly out of balance. My emotional space will be very small. I will be over-committed, undersupported, and burning out. I'll be frustrated and resentful. Tight boundaries are hard to live with for very long. Eventually I will get fed up and blow, either openly or silently. At this point I will no doubt respond by setting my boundaries at the other extreme: "I'll

never teach one of their classes again! In fact I'll leave this church and never come back. I'll never speak to them again!"

Now my emotional space is huge. It may feel like a relief for a short period, but of course it's an overreaction. The result of these boundaries is isolation and loneliness. So eventually I cool down and mellow out. I either get back to my previous commitments or I start over in a new church. But if I have not dealt with my co-dependency, I will repeat the pattern again and again.

My codependency in this case is not measured by my overcommitment but by my motivation. I'm trying to fill an emotional void within myself by seeking approval, avoiding criticism, or soothing guilt. My personal boundaries change depending upon which emotions are stimulated.

Codependent Family History

How does an individual's family of origin contribute to co-dependency? What is a codependent's family history like? In the last chapter we examined the concept of dysfunctional families, in which the basic needs of a child were not met. For the codependent, the primary unmet needs are emotional: love, acceptance, nurturance, affirmation. These unmet needs create emotional voids that affect the child's perspective in many ways.

Young children are always egocentric. This means that their view
of the world is very small—so small that they are the center of it.
When I was a child and our family drove somewhere in the evening,
I assumed the moon followed us home and stayed there—egocentric. When Mr. Rogers says, "Hello, my friend!" the young child
replies, "Hi, Mr. Rogers!" As far as she is concerned, Mr. Rogers and
she had a chat—egocentric. For the young child, the whole world
is an extension of the self.

This egocentric perspective gives children a cause-and-effect experience in all that they do and is a major factor in the dysfunctional
family's influence on a child. It tends to amplify and intensify the
impact of other issues. Since the world is an extension of themselves children perceive themselves as the cause of whatever happens in their world. They think, "If Daddy is angry, it's because I
have been naughty," or "Mommy is sad because I hurt her feelings."
A child isn't able to understand that factors far beyond them affect
these things. Children, in their limited perspective, take responsibility for things far beyond their control: "If only I behaved better,
Mom and Dad wouldn't fight"; "If only I were nice, Mommy would
like me"; "If only I were quieter, Daddy would come home and play
with me"; "If only I could try harder, do more, be better . . . then
everything would be okay"—egocentric.

The result of this illusion of control for the child in a dysfunctional family is guilt. "When things don't get better, it's my fault."
The child tries harder and harder and as is usually the case, things
don't get better. So the child silently takes responsibility and guilt
festers.

Like so many other family traits, codependency is passed from
generation to generation. Codependent parents produce codependent children. In a healthy family, appropriately met emotional needs
give children the ability, skills, and preparation to meet the needs of
their children. In a dysfunctional family, the opposite is true.

In a codependent family, neither parent is adequately available
to meet a child's needs for nurturance. If Dad is an alcoholic or is
chronically depressed, Mom is preoccupied with Dad's drinking or
depression. She's busy trying to fix the situation or hide it from the
world or both. Mom may love the child, but on a practical level she

is just as unavailable as Dad. The child emerges from that family with a hunger for love and nurturance and a lack of skills to develop intimate relationships with others. They in turn develop codependent relationships in their families and the legacy passes on.

In many codependent families the picture becomes even more complex than this. Rather than filling the child's needs, the parents are trying to draw love and nurturance *from* the child. Instead of modeling love as giving, love becomes a distorted pattern of manipulating, demanding, earning, receiving. The child's egocentric perspective of this love is "If I can only work hard enough, then I'll be lovable."

Codependents carry this pattern of egocentric solutions into adult relationships. Always looking for a way to "do it right," they build relationships with emotionally needy people who can play the role so familiar to the codependent. It's the same song, next verse: "If I can just be a better husband, she'll stop drinking." "If I can just be a better wife, he won't need other women." But no matter how they try, they just can't be quite good enough. They continue the pattern of grasping for love and acceptance.

Unwritten Rules

The unwritten rules in the codependent's family of origin are fairly predictable. These rules, though unspoken, control the emotional climate of the home. As with most unwritten rules, family members are seldom aware they exist until some distance from the family is achieved.

The rules affecting codependency tend to be rigid and unbending. They focus on the emotional atmosphere of the home rather than on the needs of the family members. They also tend to repress open communication rather than foster honesty and closeness.

In a compilation of articles titled *Co-Dependency,* Robert Stubby and John Friel do an excellent job of illustrating the connection between unwritten rules and codependency:

> Let's look at perfectionism for a moment. It is okay to expect things to be done correctly most of the time. We try to put the garbage in the garbage can, for example, rather than putting it out on the

lawn. But we see many people being downright unhappy because they expect every minor detail to go exactly as they had planned. And when we grow up in perfectionistic families, we tend to be perfectionistic, too, because it's all we know. When Dad yells and screams about a thousand little things, Mom and Dad yell at each other for minor household tasks left undone, then we begin to believe that it is very bad to leave minor things around the house undone. In fact, we eventually begin to believe that each little mistake that we make in life is a major tragedy. In extreme cases, it's not too long before we begin saying to ourselves over and over, "If only I hadn't been born. If only I were smarter or prettier or more athletic or more, more something, then everything would be okay." It's hard to feel good about ourselves when we judge everything we do as not measuring up to someone else's standards.

Basically, how we treat ourselves and others is a direct result of the rules we learned to follow as we were growing up. How we handle things like stress and conflict as adults is the result of how we learned to handle them as kids. How we choose to handle them in the present is up to us. Let's examine some of these rules which keep us stuck in codependent patterns of living.

1. It's not okay to talk about problems.
2. Feelings should not be expressed openly.
3. Communication is best if indirect, with one person acting as messenger between two others (triangulation).
4. Unrealistic expectations—be strong, good, right, perfect. Make us proud.
5. Don't be "selfish."
6. Do as I say, not as I do.
7. It's not okay to play or be playful.
8. Don't rock the boat.

If you look more carefully at these rules, you will begin to see that they all have something to do with protecting or isolating oneself from others by not taking the risk to get close. People growing up according to these rules don't realize that there are actually many families that do allow each individual to talk about problems outside the family, or to express emotions openly, or to make mistakes without undue criticism. They don't realize that in many families, being vulnerable and asking for help is both routine and okay. That isolating and denying oneself is not the best way to be.[2]

The Addictive Cycle

An addictive cycle perpetuates and intensifies compulsive behaviors and codependent relationships. The addictive process is an attempt to deal with emotional needs through behavior. Illustrated, the process looks like this:

Let's explain each of the five points.

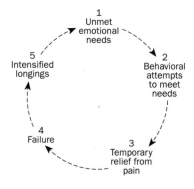

1. The basis of the cycle is the unmet emotional needs from the individual's family of origin. These emotional voids result in feelings of loneliness, emptiness, and inadequacy.
2. The attempts to meet these are identifiable symptoms: compulsive work, spending, cleaning, anger, codependent relationships, alcohol or drug abuse. All are attempts to relieve the painful feelings.
3. Each of these attempts is effective superficially and temporarily. The feelings are masked by the symptom: the alcoholic gets drunk, the addict gets high, the compulsive gets preoccupied, and the codependent has a diversion. These attempts are dysfunctional; they don't work. Because the individual's perception is skewed from childhood, however, these methods *feel* correct at the time. They give temporary relief while the codependent continues the cycle.
4. The effectiveness of the dysfunctional behavior quickly disappears, and the individual is faced with yet another failure.
5. This results in the intensification of the longings that began the cycle. The desire is for more of whatever relieved the feelings previously.

2. Robert Stubby and John Friel, in *Co-Dependency: An Emerging Issue* (Deerfield Beach, Fla.: Health Communications Inc., 1984), 34–35.

The addictive cycle is fed by denial. Denial is an unwillingness, sometimes conscious but most often unconscious, to identify and face the real source of the problem. Denial is not a contrived attempt to present a false impression; it is a distortion of reality. The individual has learned to lie to himself or herself and has learned to believe the lies.

Remember that this system, though inadequate, has been the codependent's primary method of meeting emotional needs. If he or she eliminates these methods, the codependent may feel that he or she is without options. Like a junkie lying for his pusher, a codependent needs to "protect the supply." Denial serves this purpose. So the codependent learns to view negligent parents as "actually very loving" or an abusive husband as "caring, deep down inside." Generally, codependents and adult children have spent a lifetime burying the truth, unaware they are doing it. They are "in denial."

Nothing can change in the addictive cycle until denial is broken. This is a choice only the codependent or adult child can make. A crisis of some sort is almost always necessary to initiate a change in the cycle. Denial is not usually broken when the compulsive spender has just found a great deal, but when bankruptcy looms. Not when the abused woman is in love, but when she's been beaten and abandoned. Fortunately or unfortunately, pain is an excellent motivator.

Janet's Denial

Janet grew up as the eldest of three children in a fairly stormy home. Her parents' marriage was a long series of blowups and separations. Her two younger brothers grew up with very little stability or security aside from their relationship with their big sister. Because her parents were generally preoccupied with their careers and their marital conflicts, Janet took over many parenting responsibilities for the boys. From early elementary school she cooked many meals, helped with homework, settled disputes, enforced discipline, and listened to hurt feelings. She played the part of "junior mom" very well. As a result she received a great deal of praise from her parents and other adults. When Janet left home at age twenty-two, she began to notice patterns in her life that disturbed her. While she was very successful in her job as a restaurant manager, her personal relationships were dissatisfying. The men she was attracted to inevitably turned out to be irresponsible and manipulative. The emotional investment she gave to her relationships was seldom, if ever, returned. Being "dumped" for another woman had become a too-familiar experience. Janet had dated several men who had seemed very "together." Although they expressed interest in her, Janet had found them to be boring and "cold." Although she liked them, she could never imagine becoming romantically involved with them. In her own words, "There was never any 'spark.'"

Then she met Tony. Tony was a tall, good-looking sales representative for a large company. After several months of professional acquaintance, Tony asked Janet out and she accepted. From the first date Janet was impressed. His spontaneous exuberance seemed the perfect balance to her structured, disciplined approach to life. She appreciated his outlook as well as his openness with her. Tony was a recovering alcoholic, with several years of sobriety. He shared openly regarding his struggles and feelings. This relationship felt like something Janet had always been searching for.

Janet and Tony dated steadily for two years before getting married. Although their relationship had ups and downs, both agreed that it was the best either had ever had. At times Janet felt that Tony's expectations for her were a little too high, yet with a little more effort on her part, she could measure up. Tony's subsequent approval was extremely satisfying for Janet.

A few months after their wedding, things seemed to change. Their open communication seemed to close down. Tony began spending more and more time away from home. His outlook became increasingly negative. Though she was becoming increasingly depressed about her marriage, Janet put a great deal of energy into being positive and "up" for Tony. During their second year of marriage, Tony went through seven jobs, being fired from each one for poor performance or irresponsible behavior. During this period Janet took a second job to keep the bills paid. During their third year Janet found out that Tony was drinking again and had been for some time. With great effort and expense Janet got her husband into a drug-treatment program. Tony insisted there was no need for it. Halfway through, he dropped out of the program. Within a month Tony was drinking again.

Janet came to see me to get help with Tony's problem. She was surprised and somewhat annoyed when our sessions focused on her role in the relationship. Reluctantly she agreed to take an honest look at herself and her family history. While exploring her past, Janet began to see that her parents had been overwhelmed by family responsibilities. Parental approval for Janet was a response to her ability to take over their roles and protect them from failure. By taking care of her brothers, she was also taking care of her parents.

During this process Janet discovered that she had played a parental role in each of her relationships. Her tendency to rescue and nurture was very strong, as was her need to please everyone. The flip side of this pattern was her tendency to minimize, neglect, and ignore her own needs. Janet began to see the imbalance this created. The "hero" in her required someone to rescue. Her overresponsibility fostered irresponsibility and dependence in those close to her. As Janet discovered these traits, she began to commit herself to letting them go.

The situation with Tony eventually improved, but not before it got worse. As she stopped her rescuing, Tony increased his drinking. Without her "parenting" he made some very poor decisions. Among other things, he left her, lost yet another job, and spent time in jail on a DWI charge. Only after ten months in a court-ordered alcohol-treatment program did Tony find the motivation to change. During this time Janet became involved in a support group through her church. Through the loving acceptance and accountability of these friends she began to see that her value did not depend on her ability to rescue others. As she grew spiritually, she found ways to accept God's approval and provision for her emotional needs.

Eventually Janet and Tony got back together. Over the course of a year both were able to make significant changes in the familiar roles each played in the marriage. Progress was slow and often painful, but both partners decided that the personal growth was worth the effort. Today, five years later, they are reaping the benefits of that difficult labor with a marriage and family that is satisfying to both of them.

Biblical Codependency

Codependency is an understandably uncomfortable topic for many Christians. This often comes out when I speak to church groups. Join me in a conversation I've had a number of times: Following my presentation someone stands to ask a question. It's usually a man; we'll call him Harold.

"Now wait just a minute," Harold says. "The Bible teaches us to serve others, turn the other cheek, and all that. It's godless, humanistic psychology that teaches us to look out for number one, to be self-centered. What you're calling codependency looks to me like selfless, biblical servanthood. I don't see the term *codependency* anywhere in Scripture."

"I can see what you're saying," I reply. "Your concern is certainly well-founded. Before we draw any hasty conclusions, let's take a look at Scripture. First, let's make sure you and I agree on some basics. Was Jesus selfish?"

"Of course not. He was the Son of God and died on the cross for us," Harold replies.

"I agree with you there. Was he a well-adjusted, emotionally balanced human being?" I ask.

"Sure. He was perfect."

"I agree. Did he care for himself, take care of his own needs?"

"Uh, I guess so. He probably did."

"I think so too. Did he *always* serve others?"

"Well . . . sure he did, didn't he?"

"Was he codependent?"

"Uh, I don't think so."

"Harold, I agree with you that Jesus was perfect. He is our example of ideal psychological and emotional adjustment. This is true not only in his teaching but also in his lifestyle. In John 5 Jesus healed a man at the pool of Bethesda. A fabulous miracle. But then he turned his back on all the other people who were there in need of healing and walked away. Why did he do that?"

"I don't know."

"Neither do I, but he did. How many other times did he walk away from opportunities to minister?"

"I don't know."

"That would be worth finding out. I'd encourage you to read through the Gospels and count them sometime. In Matthew 10 Jesus instructed the disciples to go into the cities to preach the gospel. What did he tell them to do if the people wouldn't listen?"

"To leave, and shake the dust off their feet."

"Exactly. He also told them to take back the blessing they gave when they arrived. That could sound almost vengeful, but Jesus was forgiving, not vengeful. Jesus was teaching his disciples to recognize the limits of their control. He taught them not to burn themselves out on an audience that wasn't responsive. Would you call that selfish?"

"No. Well, I mean, kind of, but not really."

"That's probably worth thinking about. Was it selfish for Jesus to leave a multitude of needy people to go off by himself?"

"Well, probably not."

"I agree with you. Especially since Jesus is our example of perfection. But he did just that a number of times. That could certainly *look* selfish if we didn't know better. Actually, I think Jesus was just taking good care of himself because he knew what he needed. In John 17:4, on the night before his crucifixion, Jesus said he'd finished the job he came to accomplish. That's an amazing statement considering the number of suffering people around. How could he say that?"

By now Harold is sitting down and doesn't answer.

"Jesus knew his own limits. His life was committed to serving others. Yet he did not allow the demands of others to control his life. He lived consistently according to his values and priorities even when no one else seemed to understand them. He was not selfish or self-centered, but he took care of himself. He completed the job he came to accomplish, but by many external standards, he wasn't done yet."

Many other passages of Scripture are appropriate to the issue of codependency. The familiar story of Mary and Martha in Luke 10 is a great example of Christ's response to codependency. Here we see Martha looking pretty compulsive. She was probably a first-born lieutenant in her family. She's working hard, serving others and doing good, correct things. Then there's Mary, probably the lastborn family mascot. She's being served by both Martha *and* Jesus. I can hear the local critics now: "Can you imagine that? Why that lazy so and so . . . There she is, doing nothing, taking up Jesus' precious time. And there's her poor sister working her fingers to the bone—alone!" The comments aren't too much different from what you'd hear today!

Martha asked Jesus to intervene with Mary. She expected Jesus to pat her on the back and confront Mary. Instead Jesus did the opposite. He addressed their choices and priorities rather than their external behavior. Sometimes the key to distinguishing appropriate from inappropriate behavior is motivation.

Changing Codependent Patterns

Exploring codependency often brings strong feelings toward our parents, some pleasant, others unpleasant. To understand objectively the unmet needs in your past, it is important to focus on the situation you experienced, not on the person who caused it. If you are looking for what your parents did or didn't do for you, you will probably be either defensive or bitter. Neither mind-set will help resolve anything.

Childhood needs often go unmet, not from malicious intent but because of unpredictable circumstances, ignorance, or helplessness. If a parent dies of cancer, the child experiences abandonment—

even though it certainly isn't the parent's fault. A child whose father is shipped overseas by the military also experiences abandonment. Should we blame Dad? Probably not. If a parent is physically or mentally disabled and as a result is not affectionate, is it helpful to condemn the parent? Seldom. The important thing to realize is that a need was unmet and that the void is the root of a continuing condition. The childhood experience is what is important—not who's to blame.

The next fact you need to realize is that no human being is capable of meeting your needs completely. People will fail, regardless of their effort and motivation. Open, healthy relationships are necessary and behavioral changes are important, but long-term emotional healing and change will come only through a personal relationship with the Creator. Learning to trust God to meet your emotional needs will be the "bottom line" in recovery.

Conquering Codependency

In chapter 9, I discuss the process of altering patterns from your family of origin. Keep reading! But here I want to give these steps that are especially helpful if you have identified codependency in your life.

1. Identify the unmet needs from your childhood. This may be difficult and/or painful to do. Don't hurry. Explore your family of origin fully. Compare notes with siblings or family friends if they are available. Try to view your childhood as objectively as you can.
2. Try to identify how your life is being affected currently by these unmet needs. Look for the specific symptoms of codependency listed in this chapter. Keeping a journal can be helpful in this regard: On a daily basis, record events, feelings, reactions. Compare patterns you find with those in your family history. If you have close friends who know you well, ask them to share their insights with you.
3. Consider finding a support group to aid you. Many churches have support groups for codependency, or you may want to

call or write to one of the organizations listed in the Sources. If you are not comfortable with one support group, find another.

4. Honestly examine your beliefs and perspectives regarding yourself and relationships. Consider the expectations you hold for yourself and what you assume about others. This is a process that may come slowly.

5. Educate yourself. There are many helpful books on co-dependency. Most of them will discuss these patterns in more detail. Go to your local Christian bookstore and look for an author you trust, or ask your pastor for recommendations. I've listed several books in the Sources.

6. Begin nurturing yourself. As you become aware of critical attitudes or unreasonable demands you make on yourself, challenge them. Begin learning to parent yourself (see chapter 9). Read Romans 8 and consider how God parents us.

Your Personal Family Voyage

1. Using a scale of 1 to 10 (1=trait does not apply at all, 10=trait strongly applies), rate yourself on each of the seven characteristics of codependency in this chapter:

Discontentedness
Blame
Guilt
Overresponsibility
Control
Approval
Extremes

2. Rate each of your parents on each characteristic.

3. How would your closest friend rate you?

4. How many people do you consider to be at least moderately close friends?

5. Of these, how many would you say have significant struggles in relationships?

6. How many of these depend on you as an outlet or solution for problems?

7. What percentage of your interaction with them is spent discussing problems, trials, or negative experiences?

8. Would someone who didn't know you look at these responses and consider you codependent?

9

Discarding Excess Baggage

In Christ we have the power
to overcome the negative past
with its undesirable character traits.
The cross gives us the potential
to replace them with new,
positive, healthy patterns.

Averse written to Hebrew Christians sheds more light on the journey you've been taking through your family history: "Let us also lay aside every encumbrance, and the sin which so easily entangles us, and let us run with endurance the race that is set before us, fixing our eyes on Jesus, the author and perfecter of faith" (Heb. 12:1–2).

Sorting through what you've collected in the attic is only the first step of the journey. At some point you must set aside the parts of the family collection that are causing you harm. It doesn't happen all in one day. Often you are able to take only one small box at a time to the garbage heap—only to find, much to your horror, that you run out to the dump to pick through it again. You ask yourself, *"Can I really live without this family 'treasure'? Wait—it's not a treasure, it's fool's gold. And yes, I can live without it."*

Discarding Resentment

Some of the heaviest weight to unload is that of resentment. In fact, many people are prevented from journeying anywhere because they are unwilling to discard the load of bitterness from the past.

The object of animosity may be a parent, sibling, authority figure, or some other significant person from the past. You attempt to "get them back" by withholding love or approval, withdrawing, being uncooperative, ruminating on your anger, or severing the relationship altogether. You may have denied or buried your anger so long that you aren't even aware of your bitterness, but the emotion is expressed in a variety of ways:

Unmerited explosions of anger.
Avoidance of certain individuals.

A strong desire for vengeance or retaliation.

A pessimistic or critical outlook on life.

Sarcasm, cynicism, or critical attitudes toward individuals or situations.

Overreactions or underreactions out of proportion to the current situation.

In harboring resentment you suffer more than anyone else—anxiety, tension, regret, and isolation as well as physical effects such as headaches, high blood pressure, and digestive problems. The offending individual may not even be aware of or affected by your indignation.

Many people spend their lives unwilling to release the resentment they carry from past hurts. In spite of personal suffering and relational loss they continue to seek some sort of emotional revenge on the offender. In his book *Making Peace with Your Past,* H. Norman Wright addresses this unwillingness to let go:

> Many of us live with one foot on the road of wanting to forgive and the other on the road to wanting revenge. We are immobilized. Why not make a commitment one way or the other? Why divide your energy? Why be halfhearted?
>
> If the part of you that wants revenge is stronger than the forgiving part of you, then how are you going to get revenge? Does the other person know that you resent him? Is he aware of your craving for some sort of vengeance? Have you written out your plan of vengeance, with specific details of what you plan to do? Have you bluntly told this person about your feelings and your specific plan to get back at him? If not, why not? If revenge is what you want, why not get it over with and free yourself so your life can be full and unrestricted?
>
> Your reaction is probably, "What a ridiculous idea! How could you suggest such a radical and unbiblical idea? I would never want to do that, and even if I wanted to, I couldn't do it."
>
> Really? If that is true, then why not give up your resentment completely and be washed clean of your resentful feelings?
>
> If you forgive that significant person from your past, it means you will change your response from distrust and resentment to that of love. Love frees you to disagree with what another person says or

does without becoming resentful. It even gives you the freedom to determine how much you are involved in that person's life. You can learn to communicate in an honest way and not be hooked into old patterns. The change in your attitude may help the other person change. And if it doesn't, the person may choose to back off from your relationship when he discovers you can no longer be pushed and manipulated.[1]

The resolution of resentment is forgiveness. When we choose to forgive another person, we receive the primary benefit—the freedom to choose our responses and commitments to others, to ourselves, and to God.

Our model of forgiveness is God. Each one of us has broken God's laws and erected barriers in our relationship with him. The offenses are ours, not God's. God's forgiveness is not based on his denial of our sin; he is very aware of our offenses against him. God's forgiveness is not the result of his ability to pretend that we never committed any wrong. The forgiveness our heavenly Father offers is based on his willingness to bear the cost of our sin. Christ's death on the cross was the payment for our sin. Because of that payment, God is free to respond to us as a gracious loving Father rather than as a righteous judge.

When we decide to forgive someone who has offended us, we must choose to bear the cost of the wrong committed against us. Once we forgive, we no longer require a payment for the offenses we experienced. We cancel the debt by accepting the offense. In essence, we pay the debt owed us. We no longer punish the offending person through anger, silence, avoidance, or criticism. This process frees us from the burden of resentment and allows us to let go of troublesome patterns from the past.

If we are going to unload baggage from our past, it will be necessary to relinquish any bitterness we may harbor. Forgiveness is necessary. Without letting go of our desire for vengeance, we trap ourselves into the patterns of the past.

1. H. Norman Wright. *Making Peace with Your Past* (Grand Rapids: Fleming H. Revell 1985), 67.

Does forgiveness mean I'll forget the offense? No. Forgiveness isn't a matter of blocking memories or denying the past. You will probably always carry a memory of the offense, but your emotional response to that memory can change as you forgive.

How long does forgiveness take? This varies a great deal. Forgiveness is a process and seldom occurs instantly. The process of forgiveness begins with a conscious decision. Once you have decided to forgive, God can begin to work in you to heal your wounds and change your perspective.

How will I know when I've forgiven this person? The result of forgiveness will be a change in attitude toward the experience and the individual. While the memory will remain, the experience of that memory will become a recalling of history rather than a current experience of anxiety, anger, or hurt.

How do I start forgiving? Forgiveness begins with a decision. Once you've decided to forgive, prayerfully ask God to soften your heart and broaden your understanding of this experience from your past. As you sincerely look to him, he will be faithful to shape you into his image in this area.

You may find it helpful to try to learn about the other person's history or perspective. Often our empathy grows as we understand another's experience and point of view. What was the person's family of origin like? What pain has he or she experienced? In what ways has his or her own perception been distorted?

Try to identify ways God has used your experience as a positive influence in your life. In what ways have you grown through it? How has it deepened your insight of yourself, the experience of others, or God? Could there be benefits from this experience that you haven't realized yet? Discovering how God works all things together for good (Rom. 8:28) is a major step toward healing the pain of the past.

Confronting Painful Memories

I find that many people, well on their way to sorting through and even discarding some of the baggage they've collected, come upon one or more "boxes" that they feel they just can't open. Certain painful events sit there, closed to examination. It's easier to pretend the box doesn't exist than to face the pain the contents will churn up. Let me encourage you to open the box, because once you've confronted those painful memories, they lose their power. In some ways the process and purpose of digging up and sorting through painful scenes from the past can be compared to the experience of watching a horror movie. The purpose of a horror film is to elevate the audience's anxiety level. These movies trigger an emotional response of fear and discomfort that some people find entertaining. But these films are only effective to the degree that you identify with them. When they "feel" real, you react emotionally. When you leave the theater after one or two viewings, the emotional impact is intense enough that it stays with you. Whenever you recall the movie, you'll experience similar emotions and relive the experience.

But if you sit through the movie fifty times, the experience will be quite different. Eventually you will begin to experience the film more realistically. You discover flaws in the makeup and scenery. You hear mistakes in the script and see where the plot is weak. You experience the film as a projection on a screen rather than as something currently happening to you. Your perspective becomes grounded in your current reality; it's no longer driven by your emotions.

Similarly, your painful memories may cause incredible and unpleasant discomfort the first few times you mentally walk through them. But once you've confronted them, they lose their immediacy. Conversely, as long as you expend effort trying to avoid a memory it will retain its vivid reality and negative power, even if in your dreams or in the far corner of the haunting attic you try to pretend doesn't exist.

If you have become aware of specific experiences from the past that you cannot face, consider finding a professionally trained Christian counselor to stand by you as you "take the lid off" the box. For many this is the key to unlocking stubborn patterns and opening the door to beneficial life changes.

Faith versus Feeling

Think again of being in a movie theater. Although you may identify with what's happening on the screen, it is not actually happening to you. On an intellectual level you know this, even though
you *feel* frightened—or sad or angry—on behalf of an actor or actress.

In this context you can identify a difference between *thinking* or
knowing and *feeling*. But as a counselor I often work with people
who haven't learned to distinguish between what they *feel* and what
they *think*. Let's take a brief look at the theoretical differences
between an intellectual and an emotional reaction and the choices
we make based on what we believe versus what we feel.

The Intellectual Function: What You Believe. Your intellectual function is literally what your mind does. This includes your beliefs,
values, and perspectives and is the result of cognitive learning. On
this level you evaluate, assess, and choose options based on information collected and stored in your conscious memory. All of your
conscious decisions are made on this level.

Scripture has a great deal to say regarding our intellectual function. What we choose to believe will, in many ways, affect us eter-
nally. Faith, trust, and hope are all decisions made by the intellect.

The Emotional Function: What You Feel. Emotions are your physio-
logical reaction to your perceptions—heart rate, blood pressure,
adrenaline, muscle tension, and so forth. Emotions are what your
body does in response to what you believe is happening to you.
Your perceptions play a powerful role in your emotional responses.

Emotions are morally neutral, neither right nor wrong. The Bible
neither commands nor condemns our emotions, although it has a
lot to say about our behavioral response to them. Emotional patterns are very tenacious and stubborn. Emotional change is slow
and requires patience and motivation.

Emotions are influenced by many things—environment, health,
diet, hormones, energy level, and most significantly, personal history. Since a variety of factors influence your emotions, they frequently "lie" to you. You may feel guilty when you've done nothing to be ashamed of. You may feel fearful when there's nothing

to be afraid of. You may feel defensive when no one has attacked or accused you. In each of these cases, your feelings are real—muscles tense, the heart races—and they need to be acknowledged, but they are not necessarily a reflection of what is real. They are frequently a response to experiences and patterns from the past. These emotions are a reflection of what was real long ago, a way of adapting to a situation in your childhood. That situation may no longer exist, but the emotional patterns remain. By allowing these emotions to drive your behavior, you reinforce them and they continue.

The Behavioral Function: How You Act. How you feel and/or what you think have consequences. They influence your behavior. In technical terms behavior is the external outcome of your choices (intellectual function) in response to your internal reactions (emotional function).

Behavior is not only a reaction, but a reinforcer. Since what you feel and what you believe frequently differ, you may act on one or the other. As you repeat behaviors, the pattern of your actions is reinforced or strengthened. Habits then develop without your awareness.

Scripture, of course, has a lot to say about how we conduct ourselves. Behaviors can most definitely be right or wrong, good or bad. Sometimes the appropriateness of a behavior is measured by its consequence. For example, confronting another person may be right or wrong, depending on its impact and outcome. Adultery, on the other hand, is always wrong regardless of who knows about it or how an individual may feel about it. It is a violation of God's law as well as of the marriage commitment.

The Bible makes it clear that our *minds*, not our feelings, are to be the key factor in how we live.

> Do not be conformed to this world, but be transformed by the renewing of your mind, that you may prove what the will of God is, that which is good and acceptable and perfect (Rom. 12:2).
> Finally, brethren, whatever is true, whatever is honorable, whatever is right, whatever is pure, whatever is lovely, whatever is of good repute, if there is any excellence and if anything worthy of praise, let your mind dwell on these things. The things you have

learned and received and heard and seen in me, practice these things; and the God of peace shall be with you (Phil. 4:8–9).

When you don't distinguish between what you experience emotionally based on your past and what you know as truth, you end up reverting to old patterns that can wreak havoc in relationships.

Are you a family mascot still trying to be taken care of or directed? Are you a family scapegoat still getting attention for failure? Are you still obeying some unwritten rule that doesn't apply anymore? These are all *emotional patterns* from your past that must be separated from what you know, believe, and value today before they can become a part of history where they belong.

The purpose of your family voyage is to become aware of these emotional patterns. It is important to identify which of your emotional experiences are historical and which are current. In doing so you can begin to separate what you know is true from what you feel.

Acting on Beliefs not Feelings

When Anna came to my office for an appointment, I recognized her by name. Though we had never met, she was well known in local Christian circles, active and respected for both church and community activities. Anna was an attractive woman in her mid-thirties, stylishly dressed, articulate yet soft spoken.

After we had exchanged pleasantries, she stated her first concern. "This is all confidential, isn't it?" My explanation of the legal limits of professional confidentiality seemed to settle her anxiety.

"I've gotten myself into a terrible mess," she said. Tears welled up in her eyes. "I could lose my marriage, my family, my friends at church, everything. I don't know how or why it started, and I don't have a clue what to do about it." She went on to describe her relationship with a married man in her church. What began as a committee partnership ended in a sexual affair.

Anna described how the man had been struggling with his teenage children and an uncooperative wife. She felt a great deal of compassion for him. During their long conversations, her insight and advice helped him tremendously. She felt very good about being able to help him, and he was always deeply grateful.

"I don't think I'm in love with this man, and I don't want to leave my marriage," she explained. "When he started making advances toward me, I didn't know how to respond. I knew it was wrong, but I didn't want to hurt him. I know his needs aren't met in his marriage, but neither are mine. On one hand this relationship feels good; on the other, it feels terrible."

"Could you tell me about your marriage, Anna?" I asked.

"I work hard at trying to be a good wife to Joe, even though I fail a lot," she said. "He struggles with self-esteem and isn't comfortable in social situations. That's why he doesn't come to church, though I know he's a Christian. He doesn't express it much, but in his heart he's a very loving man. At times I'm frustrated because he's not more involved with the family, but I know he's tired. As an electronics technician, his days are long. I'm sure he'd be more willing if I didn't nag him so much."

"How did you and Joe meet?" I asked.

"We met in high school," she replied. "I dated a number of boys who were very attracted to me and seemed very much in love with me. Unfortunately, the feelings were never mutual. When I met Joe, I really liked him, even though he was a little distant. The chemistry was right. I thought I was in love with him. Sometimes I think that maybe I was attracted to him because he needed me. I do believe he's a good man though, and a really nice guy."

Next we went on to discuss Anna's family history. She remembered her family of origin as moderately happy. She described her father as a very loving man who worked hard for his family. He was a very successful executive, in a job that kept him away from home for weeks at a time. When he was in town, it wasn't unusual for him to work seven-day weeks, ten to twelve hours a day. "I can remember missing Dad, wishing he were home more," Anna said. "I would write him cards and make him gifts. But, of course, his type of job required a lot."

Like Anna, her mother was an active woman. A committed Christian, she was devoted to church involvement. "For as long as I can remember, she was always doing something for some-one. Classes, committees, Bible studies, causes. All this and work-ing besides. She was amazing. Everyone was grateful that Mom was there for them."

Between the lines of Anna's story was a young girl whose par-ents avoided parenting. They weren't physically abusive, and her maintenance needs were very well met. Yet there was a gap-ing hole in the area of her emotional needs. She grew up with the subtle message that she was never quite as important as other things—work, church, other people. These busy, successful people were emotionally unavailable parents.

Anna's memories were of a harmonious home. She had very few recollections of family conflict because Mom and Dad avoided each other. In so doing, they also avoided their daugh-ter. While overt conflict was minimal, the underlying resentment was picked up by this child: "I was always trying hard to please Mom and Dad. I wished we could spend more time as a fam-ily, but there was always so much to do."

"They say that you marry your father. But not me," Anna said. "Dad was a fast-lane corporate man, very successful but never content. Joe is very content with a stable, predictable schedule and a limited future. I don't mean that critically; he does meet our needs financially. If only he'd do something at home besides sit in front of the tube."

In viewing these men in her life, Anna was seeing only a part of the picture. Dad and Joe may have been different profession-ally, but relationally they were twins. Both were afraid of inti-macy. Both were emotionally crippled men who avoided rela-tionships. Anna had married a man with whom she could continue her quest for acceptance. With Joe, Anna could once again try to be "good enough" to be loved.

During the next few sessions we began to explore Anna's situ-ation in light of her past. It all made sense to her—the unmet needs, the search for approval, the unhealthy relationships. She was ready to make a change in her life, but she could see that change would be difficult. Preparing to make these changes took several months.

For Anna it began with deciding to trust God to meet the needs no one had met for her. This was hard. Until now, trusting God had been an intellectual exercise for Anna. This would mean choosing emotional vulnerability.

To help her walk in a new direction Anna made a commitment to a support group. She needed people who would be committed to her changes, confront her honestly, hold her accountable for her changes, and love and accept her when she failed.

Her first behavioral change was honesty. She ended the affair and confessed her adultery to Joe. Her worst fear was realized; Joe left her. Anna was surprised by her own response. While it felt as if life were over, she did not beg him to stay. She was willing to believe that God would not abandon her.

Within two weeks Joe returned. Anna explained her desire for personal changes and asked Joe to be a part of them with her. He reluctantly agreed, and they began marriage counseling together.

After several years Anna and Joe are still in process, though therapy sessions are only occasional. Anna is learning to expect more out of a relationship with a man. She does less for Joe than she used to, but her motivation is very different today. She is committed to intimacy, not just maintenance. Joe is changing too. He's facing his own needs, and his perspective of love is very different from before. Together they're learning to express needs clearly and give love *to* each other, rather than trying to draw it *from* the other.

In spite of their struggles and pain, they'll both tell you they wouldn't trade the experience for anything. They are more in love now than ever. They're going to be just fine.

Reparenting

When we leave our childhood homes, most of us take over where our parents left off. We emotionally parent ourselves and continue the process they began with us. We apply their attitudes, reactions, and messages to ourselves as adults.

If our parents were critical or demeaning, we hear ourselves thinking:

"That was stupid, how could you do such a thing?"
"You'll never be able to do it right, you'll always blow it!"
"Can't you do anything right?"

These inner conversations not only reflect the critical parenting of our past, but they also keep our defensive, fearful, reactive emotional patterns current. We don't set them aside and move on to maturity. By subtly playing out the familiar role of our parents, we can continue to react in our own familiar role. We may hide the inner dialogue from those around us, but our behavioral responses to this continuing pattern are evident to others.

If our parents were controlling, we may exert control through passivity. We do this by procrastination, avoidance, irresponsibility, withdrawal, or forgetting. When we tell ourselves that we "should" do something, our natural reaction is to put it off, forget it, or get distracted.

If our parents were perfectionists we attempt to perform better, faster, or more perfectly in order to be accepted and approved—"I must," "I should," "I ought to." We repeat the phrases to ourselves. We become preoccupied with anxiety regarding mistakes and feel the need to control every situation.

Changing your family-of-origin patterns will require reparenting—acknowledging and challenging these inner messages and making conscious decisions to replace them with new messages (and consequently, new behaviors) that are more appropriate for your life today.

As you read each chapter of this book, you probably gained insight into your family history. But memory can be like an onion. As you peel away one layer, a new layer is evident. Don't assume your search for truth is complete. Keep looking for more "treasure," to determine whether it's "real gold" or "fool's gold."

Pruning Your Past

The emotional patterns from the past can be compared to a tree whose leaves are turning brown and dying. Dying leaves are a symptom of a problem that may have its source in the tree's leaves, branches, trunk, or roots.

If the leaves are turning brown, we pick them off and the tree looks better. This isn't a bad thing to do, and if the problem is a fungus or a parasite in the leaves, this may resolve the problem. But it won't resolve the problem if there is a parasite in the roots. If a branch dies, cutting it off will help the tree. If the parasite is in the branch, the problem is gone. But removing a branch won't dig out a problem in the roots. If a tree has a parasite destroying its root system, it will affect the entire tree. The leaves, branches, and trunk will be injured; the entire "tree system" will be affected.

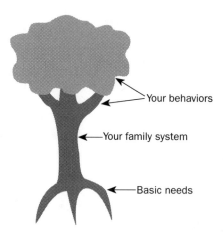

Your behaviors

Your family system

Basic needs

The parts of this tree correspond to different aspects of your emotional patterns. The leaves and branches are like the behaviors resulting from your family-of origin patterns: Jack's conflict avoidance, Hank's procrastination, Susan's relationships to emotionally distant men. Problem-causing behaviors are worth changing. For some people, these changes result in long-term life changes. This is true when habits have developed that require discipline to change or perspectives have grown that require new insights to change.

The roots of the tree correspond to basic emotional needs. Your emotional, psychological, and spiritual adjustment are dependent on how these needs are met. When these needs are not met, your life—past and present—will be affected.

The trunk of the tree can be seen as the family system in which you were raised. This is the connection between the basic needs of your past and your behavior patterns of today.

As we have discussed, some problems are more than simply behavioral habits; unmet emotional needs can cause chronic and serious difficulties. Unless these root issues are addressed, behavioral changes will be short-term and superficial, like picking brown leaves from a diseased tree. Unmet emotional needs from a dysfunctional family of origin require and deserve a great deal of time, attention, and energy to correct.

Many of us do not struggle with profound issues from our past, but instead have annoying behavioral patterns that plague our activities and relationships. These are leaves and branches that need to be pruned so that life will more fully blossom. For some of us, the assumptions we have about ourselves and our interactions with others give us trouble. If the tree is to be sound and healthy, the problem needs to be resolved at the deepest level at which it occurs.

Listening to the Past

Once you've decided to make some changes, where do you start? Change is a process that takes time. You should begin with a decision to avoid rushing through it. Many of us get the idea that in a single weekend we should be able to change patterns that have been developed and practiced over a lifetime. Don't be in a hurry to complete any of these exercises. Respond thoughtfully and write out your answers. Don't think you have to cover everything in one sitting. Feel free to stop, ponder your discoveries, and continue at another time.

Think about your family voyage. As you continue to sort through your family history, look through any family photo albums you can find. What do you see there? Do the photos invoke memories that verify or contradict your discoveries? Do memories come to mind that you haven't yet explored? If you can, talk about your family journey with siblings, extended family members, and family friends. Gather as much information from as many different perspectives as possible. Keep asking questions. As you continue your journey, consider the following questions and write down your insights.

What informal role or roles did you play in your family?
What specific behaviors were associated with these roles?

What unwritten rules are you most aware of from your family
    of origin?
What written rules did you have the most difficulty complying
    with?

What are your most vivid memories of interaction with parents
    and siblings?
What family rituals do you remember most clearly?

For what behaviors were you most often rewarded?
For what misbehaviors were you most often reprimanded?

How much do you know about your parents' families of origin?
How has their history directly affected your own development?

Based on this information and notes you made as you read each
chapter, list any current patterns in your life that you'd like to change.
Describe any problematic attitudes and behaviors as specifically as
you can. Listen carefully to your inner conversations, especially
when these problem patterns occur. Pay attention to the ways these
messages reflect the discoveries you've made on your journey. Write
out the messages you give yourself, word for word. Describe the
emotions you experience with these inner dialogues.

Over time, clearly identify the themes or patterns you discover
in your inner messages and emotions. Take some time to evaluate
each message.

What does this message say about you as a person?
Does this message have any validity in your life today?
Is this message primarily an echo from your past?

Compare these messages and attitudes to those of your heavenly Father. Since he is the perfect parent, his opinion of and
approach toward you is worth imitating. Read through the Gospels
and pay attention to the response of Jesus to various situations.
Read Romans 8 and listen to God's opinion of you as his child.

Reading the book of 1 John will help you understand the attitudes of God as your Father. Allow God to become your role model as you reparent yourself.

When you have decided that a particular message is false, write out a more correct, realistic message based on what you know, believe, and value today and remind yourself of it each time a similar situation occurs. If you need to, write yourself a cue card and carry it with you as a reminder of what you are changing in your life.

For example, if your tendency is to be self-critical and self-defeating after making a choice you regret, you may hear an inner message like: "You idiot! That was stupid. You never do anything right!"

Since these statements are untrue, challenge them directly and replace them with the truth. Your cue card may say:

> I wish I hadn't done that, but it's not the end of the world. Here's what I need to do at this point . . .
>
> or
>
> That was unfortunate, but everyone makes mistakes. What can I learn from this decision that will help me to do better in the future?

Reminding yourself of God's faithful love will also be helpful in breaking old patterns of condemnation. A reassuring passage of Scripture may say it best for you:

> Be anxious for nothing, but in everything by prayer and supplication with thanksgiving let your requests be made known to God. And the peace of God, which surpasses all comprehension, shall guard your hearts and your minds in Christ Jesus (Phil. 4:6–7).

Remember, it is absolutely essential that the new message be accurate. It is not helpful to try to convince yourself of something you know is not true simply because it sounds good.

When you have decided that a particular theme or message is problematic, formulate a plan to alter that specific pattern in your life. Practice replacing the behaviors of your past with new ones that are more appropriate for your values as an adult.

Troubleshooting

Remember that you are a part of a system. As you change, others around you will need to make changes in response to yours. You may encounter resistance and objections from family members and others who are comfortable with the old patterns. This is why it's important that you do not choose these new patterns impulsively or superficially. Prayerfully consider and choose new responses based on your priorities as an adult, not as an emotional reaction to your past. You may need to commit yourself to these changes and hold fast against outside pressure.

Try not to view people who challenge you as enemies because of their negative responses. Remember that while you are consciously choosing to change, the changes they must make in response are not their desire. Don't let their struggle stop you from growing, but consider their experience as well.

Be sure to write down any noticeable progress. Share your progress with supportive and trusted friends. Learn to enjoy your own growth. Focus on your success rather than on your difficulties. Practice being a positive, supportive, nurturing parent to yourself. You may be amazed at who you become because of your family voyage.

Your Personal Family Voyage

1. What traits or behaviors would you like to change in your life? Which would you like to strengthen?

2. What will be the most difficult aspect of change for you personally?

3. List individuals who will offer the most positive encouragement regarding the changes you are choosing to make.

4. List individuals who will struggle with and offer resistance to the changes you are choosing to make.

5. When is the most opportune time to begin making these changes?

6. Based on the approach described in this chapter, write out a specific plan for the changes you choose to make.

Appendix

A Map for the Journey

This section is on family map-making. The map is a type of family tree called a genogram. A genogram records, in picture form, information regarding a particular family: names, events, relationships, problems, and patterns. The genogram will cover at least three generations, more if you desire and can obtain the information. The purpose is to display, with a minimum of difficulty, a great deal of information about complex family patterns so that they can be viewed as a whole system in proper context.

Family therapists use genograms to summarize family structures at a glance and graphically trace family problems and patterns through space and time. In this way they are able to understand and explain habits and behaviors that would otherwise be a mystery. Because of the human tendency to repeat familiar patterns, and because of the frequency with which certain patterns occur together in relationships, family therapists can often make predictions about a family with seemingly uncanny accuracy. The genogram facilitates this skill. Your own family genogram will help illustrate how events, relationships, habits, and reactions are related to patterns that have existed in your extended family, perhaps for generations. Many of these have been communicated subtly, often without anyone's realizing it, and have been internalized as a part of your personality. Once the patterns have been identified and understood, conscious decisions can be made to retain, strengthen, or eliminate them, as we've discovered in this book.

Constructing the Map

Your genogram will be useful only if its symbols can be understood by whoever is reading it. I will suggest a legend that is helpful to me. Feel free to use my symbols, change them, or create new ones if you prefer.

To begin with, I draw women as circles and men as squares. I then write the year of the individual's birth within the symbol, using an apostrophe in place of the century (e.g., '53 instead of 1953).

'53 | Bob   ('37) Jane   In extended genograms that span several centuries I write out the appropriate numerals. I use the year of an individual's birth as opposed to a person's age so that the map doesn't become outdated quickly. To the right of the symbol, I write the person's name if I know it.

The death of an individual is indicated by an *X* drawn through the symbol with the date of death written above the symbol.

Biological and legal relationships (e.g., births, adoptions, marriages, divorces) are illustrated by vertical and horizontal lines. Two married people are connected by a horizontal line drawn between their symbols. The date of the marriage is shown by the letter *M* followed by the date, written above the line.

A disruption of the marriage is illustrated by slashes through the horizontal line. One slash indicates a separation; two slashes denote a divorce. The dates of separation and/or divorce are indicated by an *S* or *D* followed by the date. Multiple marriages and divorces are illustrated by extending the horizontal line to the left or right, whichever works better. The most recent or most significant relationship remains in the center.

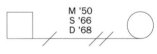

A couple who is living together outside of marriage or is involved in an extramarital affair is depicted by a dotted line.

The date they met or the date they began the relationship is indicated above the line.

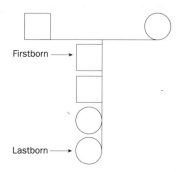

Children are depicted on a vertical line extending downward from the marriage or relationship to which they were born. The order of birth begins closest to the horizontal line and progresses downward as children are added. Many family therapists draw this aspect of the genogram with the children extending individually from the horizontal line between the parents. I've chosen this method because it gives me more room to write details about each child to the right of his or her symbol.

The following is a listing of various symbols used to illustrate a number of possible child situations:

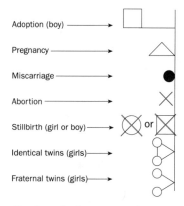

Before we go any farther, let's stop and practice reading the map. Below is an example of a hypothetical family. Before you read the description of this family, look this genogram over carefully and see how much information you are able to draw from it.

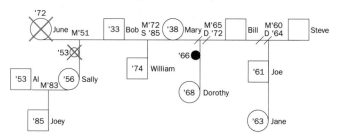

Bob (born in 1933) has been married to Mary (born in 1938) since 1972. Together they have a son, William, who was born in 1974. They have been separated since 1985.

Mary was married twice previously. She married her first husband, Steve, in 1960. They had two children together—Joe, who was born in 1961, and Jane, who was born in 1963. Mary and Steve were divorced the year after Jane's birth, in 1964. Mary's second husband was Bill, whom she married the year after her divorce, in 1965. The following year, 1966, they had a miscarriage, and two years later their daughter, Dorothy, was born. They divorced in 1972, the same year Mary married Bob.

Bob was a widower whose first wife, June, died shortly before he and Mary were married. Bob and June had been married twenty-one years. Their first daughter was stillborn in 1953, and three years later their daughter, Sally, was born. Sally was sixteen years old when her mother died and her father remarried.

Sally is the only one of the children who has married. In 1983 she married Al, who is three years older than she. Their son, Joey, was born two years later, in 1985.

Now you can begin to see how much information can be compressed into a simple drawing. You can also begin to see how complex it will get as we begin looking at three or more generations. This, of course, is just the beginning of our family map making. We have a great deal to include in a genogram.

Let's take the family map a step further and include some of the less obvious familial relationships. By now we should be keenly aware of the many varieties of emotional relationships that occur within families. Just as there are symbols for biological and legal relationships, there are also symbols for emotional relationships.

A relationship described as especially close is depicted by two parallel lines drawn between the individuals. An emotionally distant or estranged relationship is illustrated by a line broken by two ninety-degree lines. If only one person in the relationship is hostile or distant, the perpendicular

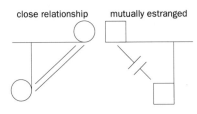

close relationship   mutually estranged

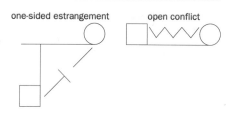

line is drawn only on that person's side of the broken line. Overt conflict is indicated by a jagged line connecting individuals.

If one particular family member is distant or emotionally isolated from the rest of the family, a line is drawn separating that person from the rest of the family.

Let's try another example just for practice.

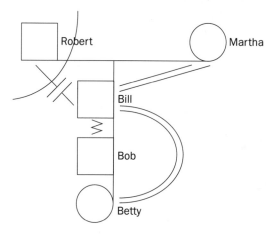

This genogram shows that Bill has very close relationships with both his mother and his younger sister, Betty, but is distant from his father. The relationship between Bill and his brother Bob is one of open conflict, and the father, Robert, is uninvolved in the family as a whole.

You'll want to add miscellaneous information that doesn't lend itself to symbols but is necessary for the understanding of a particular family. This information can be added either in the columns beside the map, with arrows indicating to whom the information applies, or by writing a brief statement next to the symbol representing the individual.

Applying the Map

You'll probably find, depending on how much detail you explore, that familiar patterns repeat themselves. Certain patterns will recur in generation after generation. Sometimes the specific behavior will differ among generations, but the emotional issue will be the same. You may find that "coincidental" events don't seem nearly so coincidental when you see them repeated over time and generations.

A good example of this type of discovery is Kathy, a twenty-six-year-old single woman engaged to be married. She had always done well in school, was an effective leader in her church, and was very successful in her position as a nurse. When she drew her genogram and briefly described her family members, it looked like this:

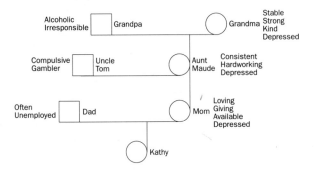

By going through the steps of drawing this family map, Kathy made an amazing discovery. The women in her family for generations were strong, successful, hardworking women married to immature, unreliable, dependent men. As we discussed earlier, people with these opposite traits tend to be attracted to one another. Furthermore, the roles of rescuer and victim were apparently reinforced generation after generation in Kathy's family: Kathy learned it from her mother, who had learned it from her mother, and so on. After discovering this pattern she sat down and wrote an honest description of her fiancé, Jim.

Jim was a twenty-two-year-old man who had been abused as a child. He had left high school in the eleventh grade to begin working as a machinist. Although he earned a good salary, he was seriously in debt and had periods of depression when he did not communicate with anyone except Kathy. Much of their conversation revolved around Jim's feelings and Kathy's insights.

Though she had never realized it before, Kathy could see that the family pattern was clearly a part of her relationship with Jim. She decided to postpone the wedding date until she and Jim could get some professional premarital counseling. Jim began dealing with his own role of victim, and Kathy discovered that she could stop rescuing if she chose. Over time each made significant changes and the relationship grew into a healthy partnership.

Other Variables

A genogram can show family patterns that are variables in individual personality development, as the example of Bob illustrates. After explaining some general family patterns, Bob's response to me was, "I must be the exception to the rules because I'm nothing like my dad. In fact, as a child I swore that I'd never be anything like my dad and that's just what happened." I responded by saying that I'd be surprised if that were true, but I'd be glad to be wrong. As Bob shared his story, I jotted down a short genogram.

Bob's dad, Robert, was a very demanding, critical man who made life quite hard at home. He was verbally and at times physically abusive to Bob. Robert had grown up in an orphanage during the Depression with very little security of any kind. Now, years later, Bob could see that his dad was an inwardly frightened man who had to control others to gain a feeling of security. Bob learned to deal with Dad by staying out of his way. He would never disagree with Dad or confront him in any way. Survival to Bob meant adapting to Dad and letting him be "right" no matter what.

Over the years these "survival techniques" became personality traits. When his son, Bobby, came along, Bob was a pushover for his firstborn. Bobby became a spoiled brat due, at least in part, to Bob's passivity. Like most children, Bobby was constantly searching for limits on his behavior and a sense of secure, predictable boundaries. Bob's passivity kept him from enforcing consistent limits on Bobby. Since having tantrums usually produced favorable results, Bobby soon became very proficient at them. The result was that Bobby grew up to become the "spitting image" of his granddad.

The men in Bob's family genogram looked like this:

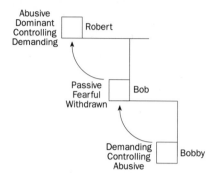

While the behavior patterns seemed to skip a generation, all of these behaviors are expressions of deep, emotional insecurity. In reality, all three generations of men were desperately insecure.

Observing Patterns

Since a family is a system, the parts fit together and interrelate as a functioning whole. In other words, the behaviors of different individuals will tend to complement one another. One will react according to the behavior of the other. For example, a very responsible, self-disciplined child will commonly have a sibling who is irresponsible and impulsive. A dominant, verbal, controlling spouse will tend to find a partner who is passive, withdrawn, and conforming.

Children tend to acquire the more pronounced traits of their same-sex parent and to be emotionally drawn to partners who have the characteristics of their opposite-sex parent. Because of these tendencies, this type of complementarity repeats itself from generation to generation. This is also why we see adult children repeating the marriages of their parents, even if they consciously would rather not.

Any known incidence of alcoholism, chemical dependency, or abuse should be clearly noted in the genogram. When these occur, pay close attention to the informal roles chosen by the other family members as you look for patterns. Based on the information from the chapter on family roles, you may be amazed at the unspoken information that jumps out at you.

Let's look at another genogram. This one is of a well-known family, the Roosevelts.[1]

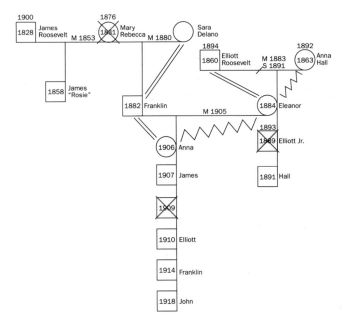

In the family of Eleanor Roosevelt, the pattern was one of mother-daughter resentment and close feelings between father and daughter. Although both parents had died by the time she was eleven, Eleanor remembered having a special relationship with her father while feeling her mother was harsh and insensitive to his predicament. Her father was in fact an alcoholic and quite irresponsible, and her mother had once committed him to an asylum and later separated from him. In the next generation, the daughter, Anna, a firstborn like Eleanor, preferred her father and saw her own mother as overly harsh. Throughout her adolescence she had a stormy relationship with Eleanor, which did not change until her father contracted polio.

1. Adapted from: *Genograms in Family Assessment*, by Monica McGoldrick and Randy Gerson (New York: W.W. Norton & Co., 1985), 82.

An Old Testament Family Map

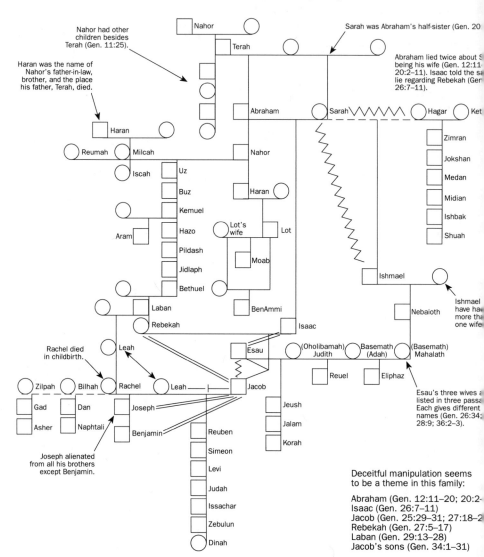

Nahor had other children besides Terah (Gen. 11:25).

Haran was the name of Nahor's father-in-law, brother, and the place his father, Terah, died.

Sarah was Abraham's half-sister (Gen. 20

Abraham lied twice about S being his wife (Gen. 12:11 20:2–11). Isaac told the sa lie regarding Rebekah (Ger 26:7–11).

Ishmael have ha more tha one wife

Rachel died in childbirth.

Esau's three wives a listed in three passa Each gives different names (Gen. 26:34; 28:9; 36:2–3).

Joseph alienated from all his brothers except Benjamin.

Deceitful manipulation seems to be a theme in this family:

Abraham (Gen. 12:11–20; 20:2–
Isaac (Gen. 26:7–11)
Jacob (Gen. 25:29–31; 27:18–2
Rebekah (Gen. 27:5–17)
Laban (Gen. 29:13–28)
Jacob's sons (Gen. 34:1–31)

Adapting the Map

Inevitably some situations in a family will not be covered by these guidelines, and others will make drawing a genogram extremely complex and confusing. Mapping such situations will require creativity on your part. Remember, the purpose of the family map is to organize information for *you*. The directions I've given have been helpful for me. If you think of a better way to do it, go right ahead! Make whatever changes you need to make the family map fit your family.

As an example of adaptation, let's take a look at the genogram of the Old Testament patriarchs Abraham, Isaac, and Jacob. In this genogram I've drawn five generations—from Terah, the father of Abraham, to the twelve sons of Jacob. This family map is complicated by the Old Testament practice of polygamy and intermarriage within family lines, as well as the large number of children. You'll also notice that many of the women in this family are not named, but their existence can be assumed. For example; Abraham's and Sarah's mothers aren't mentioned in the Bible, but we know that they existed and that they were both married to the same man, Terah (Gen. 20:12).

In a complex family like this one, we need to adapt the genogram for the sake of clarity. For example, Jacob married two sisters, Leah and Rachel. I thought that the simplest way to indicate this relationship was to move Leah to the same perpendicular line as Rachel and show both of Leah's relationships with an arrow.

The fact that Lot begat children by each of his two daughters forced another adaptation. The daughters are shown without mates and lines are drawn from Lot to where their husbands should be.

Use this genogram as an example. Take note of any new information you learn concerning the construction of the genogram. At that point you should be ready to draw your own detailed family genogram.

Sources

Beattie, Melody. *Codependent No More*. San Francisco: Harper & Row, 1987.

Berman, William B., Dale R. Doty, and Jean Huff Graham. *Shaking the Family Tree*. Wheaton, Ill.: Victor Books, 1991.

Brawand, Alice, Dave Carter, Henry Cloud, Earl Henslin, and John Townsend. *Secrets of Your Family Tree*. Chicago: Moody Press, 1991.

Co-Dependency: An Emerging Issue. Deerfield Beach, Fla.: Health Communications, 1984.

Friel, John, and Linda Friel. *Adult Children, The Secrets of Dysfunctional Families*. Deerfield Beach, Fla.: Health Communications, 1988.

Friends in Recovery. *The Twelve Steps: A Spiritual Journey*. San Diego: Recovery Publications, 1988.

Hoopes, Margaret, and James Harper. *Birth Order Roles and Sibling Patterns in Individual and Family Therapy*. Rockville, Md.: Aspen Publishers, 1987.

Leman, Kevin. *The Birth Order Book*. Grand Rapids, Mich.: Fleming H. Revell, 1985.

Leman, Kevin, and Randy Carlson. *Unlocking the Secrets of Your Childhood Memories*. Nashville, Tenn.: Thomas Nelson, 1989.

McGoldrick, Monica, and Randy Gerson. *Genograms in Family Assessment*. New York: W.W. Norton, 1985.

Roman, Mel, and Patricia Raley. *The Indelible Family*. New York: Rawson, Wade, 1980.

Sell, Charles. *Unfinished Business.* Portland, Oreg.: Multnomah Press, 1989.

Wright, H. Norman. *Making Peace with Your Past.* Grand Rapids, Mich.: Fleming H. Revell, 1985.

For names of Christian counselors in your area, contact the following:

American Association of Pastoral Counselors
9504 – A Lee Highway
Fairfax, VA 22031
(703) 385-6967

Christian Association for Psychological Studies (CAPS)
26705 Farmington Road
Farmington Hills, MI 48018
(313) 477-1350

For information regarding speaking engagements or seminars write or call:

P. Roger Hillerstrom
c/o CRISTA Counseling Service
19303 Fremont Avenue North
Seattle, WA 98133-9703
(206) 546-7215